Achieving your
Masters
in Teaching
and Learning

MTL

Achieving your
Masters
in Teaching
and Learning

Mary McAteer

with Fiona Hallett
Lisa Murtagh
Gavin Turnbull

www.learningmatters.co.uk

First published in 2010 by Learning Matters Ltd.

© 2010 Mary McAteer

British Library Cataloguing in Publication Data
A CIP record for this book is available from the British Library.

ISBN 978 1 84445 214 9

Cover design by Topics
Text design by Phil Barker
Project management by Deer Park Productions, Tavistock, Devon
Typeset by PDQ Typesetting Ltd, Newcastle-under-Lyme, Staffordshire
Printed and bound in Great Britain by Bell & Bain Ltd, Glasgow

Learning Matters Ltd
33 Southernhay East
Exeter EX1 1NX
Tel: 01392 215560
info@learningmatters.co.uk
www.learningmatters.co.uk

This book is dedicated to my father, Patrick McLaughlin, my first role model of a reflective practitioner.

Contents

Acknowledgements

Throughout my life I have been privileged to have experienced excellence and diversity in my own personal and professional learning.

Perhaps the most profound learning that I have experienced is the reciprocity between teaching and learning, and the realisation that to be a teacher is to be a learner. I owe a debt of gratitude to all those from whom I have learned; family, friends, teachers, from primary through secondary to university, colleagues, and perhaps most of all, the many wonderful students I have had the joy of teaching. They have all challenged and provoked me, supported and guided me, and in doing so, have helped me understand myself as a teacher and learner, helped me to articulate and develop that understanding, and hence continue to strive towards improving my practice. This book is written in the hope that teachers reading it may also have such pleasure and enrichment in their learning and teaching.

Before I ever heard the term "reflective practitioner", before I had even started school, I saw reflective practice in action, I knew what it was, and more importantly, I realised its significance and potency. Through this experience, I came to understand the thoughtful, questioning, and dynamic nature of the teaching-learning nexus.

Case study illustrations used in the book were drawn from practice, and generously supplied by Steve Merrill, Maggie Webster and Jane Wood.

The large case study on which the first part of Chapter 3 is based was derived from work with Jane Dewhurst, Settle College, North Yorkshire, and her A-Level Physics pupils.

The Authors

Mary McAteer

Mary has worked for the past 28 years as a teacher, holding a range of senior pastoral and curriculum posts. She has also worked as an LA CPD Provider, and Lecturer/Senior Lecturer in an HEI. Her present role is as Principal Lecturer and Programme Leader for an extensive M Level CPD Programme in the Faculty of Education, Edge Hill University, where she also holds a Teaching and Learning Fellowship.

Fiona Hallet

Fiona Hallett has a background working with students with Social, Emotional and Behavioural Difficulties and is the Programme Leader for the National Award for SEN Coordination at Edgehill University. She is also a Research Fellow of the Centre for Learner Identity Studies.

Lisa Murtagh

Lisa is the BA (Hons) Primary Education with QTS Part Time Programme Leader at Edge Hill University. She has been involved in initial teacher training for 9 years and her research interest lies with assessment for learning.

Gavin Turnbull

Gavin Turnbull is an Associate Lecturer within the Postgraduate Professional Development team at Edge Hill University. He has a background of working in a range of multidisciplinary settings and is interested in inter-professional working, risk and professional practice.

CHAPTER 1

About the Masters in Teaching and Learning

Chapter Objectives

By the end of this chapter you should have gained an understanding of:
- the background to the MTL;
- how the MTL differs from other master's programmes;
- the different roles of key individuals involved;
- the benefits of the programme.

Introduction

As a newly developed programme, much is still being written about the Masters in Teaching and Learning (MTL), and it can be difficult to get a clear overview of it. This chapter is designed to give a straightforward, brief overview of the key points that newly qualified teachers (NQT), school-based coaches, head teachers, and higher education institution (HEI) tutors will need to be aware of as they embark on planning and delivering it. It gives a brief synopsis of the background to its development, key aspects of its structure and design, and some indication of the roles and responsibilities of the personnel concerned.

Background to the MTL

The proposal to make teaching an all-master's profession is perhaps the biggest change in teacher education since the early 1980s, when a bachelor's degree became a requirement for all new teachers in the United Kingdom. For the first time, this meant that all teachers, primary and secondary, would be qualified to degree level.

In recent years, initiatives by the Training and Development Agency for Schools (TDA) have supported and funded the provision of high-quality continuing professional development for practising teachers, building on the mandatory induction requirements. Most of this professional development has been linked to master's-level work studied either in universities, or in partnership arrangements with them. The introduction of the Professional Standards for Teachers (2007) Framework, and the linking of these standards to performance review and career development have formalised the need for teachers to plan their career pathway within the Standards Framework. The TDA Strategic Plan 2008–2012 proposed that the newly developed MTL would, as a practice-based professional development qualification, build on initial teacher training (ITT), deepening and broadening professional skills while addressing individual teacher needs. While it is proposed that the qualification will ultimately be available to all teachers, the initial roll-out will be for newly qualified teachers.

Why was MTL developed?

In 'Being the Best for our Children: Releasing talent for teaching and learning' (2008a) the DCSF outlined its intention to create a new master's-level qualification in order to *boost the quality of teaching needed to improve the achievement of all pupils*. This new qualification was to be directed primarily to the needs of early-career teachers, providing additional support through induction and offering a more structured experience of early professional development. The vision was that the new programme would be practice-based, and would both develop and improve teacher quality, specifically through *enquiry and the use of evidence*. The proposed consequence for participants on the programme was the development of higher-level teaching skills, and hence the improved achievement of all pupils.

What makes MTL different from other master's programmes?

This programme was developed collaboratively with schools, local authorities, and HEIs, and was based on the concept that it would integrate the Professional Standards for Teachers while also addressing the Quality Assurance Agency for Higher Education (QAA) master's-level requirements (both of which are found in full in Appendices 1 and 2). In this way, the programme is designed to have both academic rigour and also maximum impact on practice development.

The significant feature of this new programme, which starts in January 2010 is the relationship between participants, their school and HEIs. School coaches and mentors will provide much of the ongoing support for participants, while HEIs will provide each participant with an academic tutor, who will also work closely with coaches and mentors to ensure an appropriate and coherent programme is being followed.

A further significant difference between MTL and other MA or MEd programmes is its contiguity with initial teacher training. It is designed to build seamlessly on ITT, providing high-quality early professional development in a way that develops both your practice as a teacher and your professional knowledge as an educator.

Structure and design of the MTL

You will find much more detail about the structure of the MTL in *The National Framework for Masters in Teaching and Learning*, published by the TDA in February 2009. The following section provides a summary and synthesis of the key points. The key principles which informed the development of the programme include the following and describe the programme as one which will:

- be practice-based, at master's level, focusing on teaching and learning, and lead to effective teaching so that children and young people achieve their potential, regardless of their age, gender, abilities and background;
- be centred in practice-based learning, with the range of professional learning opportunities agreed by the teacher with their coach and tutor to meet their personal, professional, career and school needs;
- be built on ITT or previous professional learning and take account of the NQT's route into teaching, or the more experienced teacher's previous professional development;
- align with induction and performance management requirements;
- be a personalised professional learning journey that is structured in three phases, providing a coherent learning experience that progressively develops, broadens and deepens each teacher's professional attributes, knowledge skills and understanding.

In addition, the programme aims to allow teachers to develop skills of enquiry, the use of evidence and research, through addressing four content areas, drawing on the skills of ICT as appropriate. Designed to be a personalised learning experience, it is intended that it can be completed within three years, and it is expected that this will be the normal timescale for teachers. MTL providers are charged with providing continuity should teachers move school or location during that period. In essence, this programme is designed to help you, as a practising teacher, to develop the skills and strategies that will support your ongoing professional development, as an effective and reflective practitioner.

This new programme has been designed to specifically meet the needs of practising teachers and allows for a high degree of flexibility and personalisation. There is a strong recognition that your needs within your school context are important starting points for further professional development and study.

In your initial teacher training, or other professional experience, you will have begun to use the skills of reflection and enquiry, and the MTL is designed to build on these, so that you become better able to use these skills in more formalised enquiry and research, and use evidence appropriately. In doing this, you will be afforded opportunities to develop, broaden and embed, and deepen your own knowledge of young people and their education, both in the school environment and beyond.

The TDA website identifies the MTL as the *only national masters programme for teachers, delivered locally, which combines all the following features.*

- *A focus on children and young people*
- *School-based learning*
- *A personalised programme*
- *Alignment with induction*
- *Higher education institution (HEI) and school collaboration*
- *A trained in-school coach*
- *An assigned tutor from an HEI*
- *Funding*

(www.tda.gov.uk/teachers/mtl/how_will_mtl_work.aspx)

The programme is designed in three phases to reflect this. These three phases build successively on previous learning, and address your needs in a structured and focused way. Each phase has its on specific principles and structures, and learning outcomes.

In addition to the three phases, there are also four content areas, which you are expected to address throughout your MTL study.

The three phases of MTL

The three phases are not equal in size or time, and are designed to emphasise the different nature of professional learning requirements and their development as you progress from NQT to early-career professional. Each phase has its own specific characteristics, and allows for the development of both professional knowledge and practice, and subject, phase or other specialism knowledge.

1. Phase 1 (worth 40 credits) the **Developing** phase, is closely aligned with the induction phase, and supports the development of skills of enquiry and the use of evidence in supporting your developing professional practice.
2. Phase 2 (worth 80 credits) the **Broadening and Embedding** phase, allows for focus on the four content areas in order to both broaden and securely embed professional knowledge, skills and understanding within the context of your own workplace.
3. Phase 3 (worth 60 credits) the **Deepening** phase, allows you to undertake a deeper study in a chosen specialist area. During this phase you will be expected to both engage in the review of existing expertise and knowledge, and also to undertake a formal enquiry into your own professional practice.

Figure 1.1 MTL phases

The four content areas

These four areas reflect the wide range of professional practice and knowledge that is appropriate in twenty-first century schools and settings. They will feature strongly in phase 2 of the MTL, providing the key focus for assessment opportunities.

1. Teaching and learning, including personalised learning, and assessment for learning.
2. Subject knowledge for teaching, and curriculum and curriculum development.
3. How children and young people develop, including behaviour management and inclusion.
4. Leadership and management, and working with others, in and beyond the classroom.

Delivery of the programme

The programme delivery will be very much a shared enterprise, drawing primarily on the expertise of school-based coaches and mentors in partnership with HEI tutors. Schools and HEIs will be equal partners in this enterprise, and will have joint responsibility for both delivery and quality of the programme. In addition, the HEI provider will draw on a range of sources of expertise, including local authorities, in order to provide the best possible practice-based learning opportunities for teachers. School-based coaches and mentors will provide in-school support and challenge on an ongoing basis, and the whole programme will be delivered in a way which enables teachers to access personalised learning opportunities. Participants, coaches, mentors and tutors will also have access to online resources and forms of communication through the use of a virtual learning environment (VLE). For you as a teacher, the triadic relationship between yourself, your mentor or coach, and your HEI tutor is the key determinant in how the route through MTL is planned to be appropriate to your professional learning needs.

Who does what?

Your HEI tutor and school-based coach or mentor will work as joint equal partners in a range of capacities to ensure that you have access to the best possible professional learning experiences. Your school-based coach or mentor has particular responsibility for working from a school and local perspective, while your tutor will work from a regional, national and international perspective. Each of them will have a clear understanding of both the Professional Standards for Teachers and the QAA master's-level requirements. In addition to these key personnel, your head teacher also plays a vital role in supporting the MTL work within your school. The specific roles in relation to the MTL are outlined below.

Your coach is the person you will be in contact with on a regular basis (possibly daily, if they are based in your school). They have lead responsibility for providing you with all the appropriate learning opportunities that will allow you to successfully complete your MTL. Working from a school and local perspective, they will also liaise effectively with the HEI tutor and be familiar with the requirements of working at master's level.

The HEI tutor provided by the HEI will have the lead role in assessing the progress of the teacher undertaking the MTL. As with the coach, the role of the HEI tutor is based on them having a clear understanding of the professional standards for teachers and the QAA master's-level requirements. Working from a regional and national perspective, the HEI tutor will work collaboratively with the teacher undertaking MTL and in a complementary role with the coach, and will take lead responsibility in assessing the master's requirements of the MTL.

Table 1.1 indicates the nature and extent of the complementary relationship between these two key people, detailing their specific responsibilities in relation to eight key aspects of your learning experience.

Table 1.1. Relationship between coach and tutor

Aspects of your learning	Role of the coach	Role of the HEI tutor
Identifying the teacher's professional needs, and planning for the next stage in their learning, drawing appropriately on induction and performance management outcomes	• Assessing, at the start of the programme, whether any M-Level credit gained in ITT can be taken forward, in line with the principles of MTL • Identifying the teacher's professional learning needs in relation to the learning outcomes for each phase of the programme	
	Taking the leading role in identifying, with the teacher, progress towards meeting the learning outcomes for each phase of the programme, determining ongoing professional learning needs for development	Working with the in-school coach and the teacher to plan HEI tutor and other expert input to provide appropriately personalised learning opportunities for the teacher, in relation to the four content areas of the MTL
Advising, providing and making accessible appropriately personalised learning opportunities for the teacher that draw on a range of expert inputs and resources in relation to the four MTL content areas	Identifying, providing as appropriate, and brokering professional learning opportunities that are available within the school and its wider context	Providing learning opportunities, beyond the school context, that draw on regional, national and, where appropriate, international expertise and resources matched to meet the teacher's needs
Providing opportunities for collaborative learning with other teachers and, as appropriate, with other members of the school and children's workforce, in the school and beyond the school	Supporting the teacher to engage in professional learning with teachers and other professionals within the school and the wider school context that focus on improving professional practice to impact on outcomes for children and young people through, for example, undertaking relevant research activities	Providing opportunities for the teacher to learn with and from other teachers on the MTL programme
Engaging in dialogue to develop the teacher's understanding of the learning experience and to move the learning on	Questioning and challenging the teacher to further develop understanding of what the teacher has learnt and help the teacher to understand how this learning could be used to improve professional practice	
Supporting the teacher's reflection on the outcomes of children and young people he or she teaches and how the teacher's practice has impacted on these outcomes	Supporting the teacher to develop and apply diagnostic skills to identify children's and young people's progress and needs and to select appropriate interventions to ensure successful outcomes	Supporting the teacher to engage with and making use of relevant theory to further develop practice
Supporting the teacher's critical analysis of a range of sources of evidence in order to improve their practice	Working with the teacher to apply and further develop the skills of enquiry and how to identify, critically analyse and use classroom-based evidence to further improve professional practice	• Introducing and engaging the teacher with a range of sources of national and international evidence • Supporting the teacher to develop and apply skills in enquiry and research
Supporting the teacher to analyse the evidence of impact of professional practice on outcomes that will be used towards the assessment and enable the tutor to make a summative assessment of achievement	Working with the teacher to analyse evidence that demonstrates the teacher's progress	
	• Supporting the teacher to identify what counts as valid evidence of pupil progress and how this can be used to demonstrate improved teacher practice • Undertaking formative assessment of the teacher's progress and provide timely feedback	Making the summative assessments
Supporting the teacher to communicate the outcomes of their research, particularly in phase 3, to contribute to the professional learning of others and supporting the teacher in planning for further professional development	Working with the teacher to identify the next career stage and subsequent professional learning needs	
	Facilitating opportunities for the teacher to share their learning to support the learning of others within the school and local context	Providing opportunities for the teacher to share and review their learning with other professionals within the wider context

The role of the head teacher

Although not charged with specific responsibilities in the provision of the MTL, head teachers will have a central role in supporting NQTs in their schools who are engaged on the programme. Funding for the MTL will come directly to the NQT's school, and so head teachers will have responsibilities in terms of the deployment of this funding to cover the costs of teachers and coaches being away from their classrooms. This is a key way in which this valuable work can be supported, and will ultimately benefit the school.

What are the benefits of the MTL?

This programme is not developed as a compulsory part of teachers' professional development. However, it is envisaged that the benefits it provides will be attractive to both teachers and their schools. As a skills and process-based qualification, rooted in professional practice development, completing it will benefit teachers in equipping them with higher-order skills, improved practice, and the attributes of, and desire for, lifelong learning. It is also recognised that the early years in teaching are the most challenging, and having in place a structured and high-level professional development programme will provide support at this vital stage, and also provide evidence for later in your career that you have actively pursued your professional development.

In addition to the benefit to NQTs, there will be professional development opportunities for existing teachers to act as coaches, participate in training, and work towards a more collaborative culture in schools and settings. Working alongside HEI tutors will also be of direct benefit to them as they become part of a broader professional community and context.

Schools in the twenty-first century are changing rapidly, and will continue to do so. The recruitment and retention of highly qualified and well motivated staff is a cornerstone in the provision of high-quality learning experiences for children and young people. The ability to work with a range of other professionals in creative, flexible ways, and to assess the impact of that work on the school and its pupils will be central in providing excellent schools for children and young people. Hopefully, your engagement with MTL will provide you with a range of rich opportunities to develop your own capacity as a twenty-first century educator.

Using this book

The book deals in turn with each of the phases, and also addresses the more generic academic skills and attributes you will develop during your study. Each of Chapters 3 to 7 is illustrated with real case studies of students undertaking postgraduate professional development activities, and in each case, references are made to academic skills and academic literature relevant to the case study.

Chapter 2 deals with phase 1 of the MTL, and as such, is a chapter that you will need to read during your NQT year. However, it is also a chapter that you might revisit to supplement your work in Chapters 3, 4, 5 and 6, each of which focuses on one of the content areas in phase 2. You can read these chapters in any order that suits your own interests and work pattern. Chapter 7 deals with phase 3, and will once again refer back to some of the generic skills introduced in Chapter 2.

Summary

In this chapter you will have:
- gained an overview of the MTL;
- understood the roles and responsibilities of key individuals in planning and delivering the programme;
- explored where to find more information about the MTL;
- understood how to use this book.

PART ONE

PHASE 1 – DEVELOPING

Getting started on your MTL

To teach is to learn twice.

(Joseph Joubert, nineteenth century)

Who dares to teach must never cease to learn.

(John Cotton Dana, nineteenth century)

Chapter Objectives

By the end of this chapter you should have:
- **a clear understanding of the professional development activities which you will engage in during your first year of teaching;**
- **an understanding of how these activities support phase 1 of your MTL;**
- **an awareness of a range of ways in which your MTL work will be assessed;**
- **an understanding of the academic rigours and conventions of reading, writing and presenting at master's level;**
- **an understanding of the concepts and complexities of practitioner enquiry.**

Introduction

As a newly qualified teacher, you have now completed one stage of your professional learning, and are about to embark on the next stage. This next phase is probably the most exciting learning journey of your professional life. Day and daily, you will find that you continue to learn about teaching, about your subject, about the organisation, structure and operation of schools and other settings, and probably most importantly, you learn about yourself. As you embark on your teaching career, you have the opportunity to formalise and maximise this learning by undertaking the new MTL qualification.

Getting started

Phase 1 of the MTL, known as the Developing phase, is worth 40 credits towards your MTL. It is designed to be congruous with your induction activities (which are compulsory), and to provide a smooth continuation of your ITT. It is designed to provide *personalised learning opportunities based on an initial diagnosis, focusing on developing skills of enquiry and use of evidence, and on professional practice in the school context.* (**www.tda.gov.uk/partners/ mtl.aspx**). Specifically, its aim is to allow you to develop professional attributes, knowledge, skills and understanding through enquiry and the use of evidence, in a new context. You may already have some master's-level credits from your Postgraduate Certificate of Education (PGCE) or other, previous study, and if so, can carry 30 of these forward. During your first year, you will be able to use the normal Career Entry and Development Profile (CEDP) activities to support these 30 credits, and some further enquiry-based activities will make up the full 40 credits of this phase. Let us now look at this phase in some more detail.

Table 2.1 shows the way in which this phase is structured, and how the necessary credits may be obtained. Teachers who already have master's-level credits take modules 1a and 2a, while those with no master's credits take modules 1b and 2b.

Induction and the MTL

As a newly qualified teacher, you are now in a position to start embedding your professional learning and enhancing your professional practice. You will move beyond the QTS standards, and develop increasing competence in the core standards. During your first year, you will have the opportunity to engage in a range of professional activities related to your own teaching. The new MTL structure now allows you to not only use this as part of your early professional development, but also integrate it into a full master's professional development programme.

By the end of this year, you should have securely embedded all the QTS standards, and be in the process of becoming confident in the core standards. These standards are benchmarks of your practice and will form part of your performance management as your career progresses. The MTL is designed to offer you opportunities to engage in activities which will help you work towards core, and indeed the higher standards, such as post-threshold, excellent or advanced. You will notice in reading these standards how the higher-level standards require a much broader knowledge base, and also, crucially, a more critical involvement with your practice.

What happens during phase 1 depends on whether you have any master's-level credits that you can carry forward into your MTL. Your school-based coach, together with your HEI tutor, will assess whether previous credit is applicable in this respect. You will need to be able to demonstrate that *through use of skills of enquiry and use of evidence that there has been previous impact of your practice on children's and young people's outcomes.* If you can use credits from your previous study, perhaps from work you did during your PGCE year while on placement, then you will be able to build on this work to complete the other 10 credits required for this phase. These further 10 credits may be achieved by using your work during induction, and reflecting on it, assessing the ways in which you now are developing your practice and impacting on children's and young people's learning.

Table 2.1 Structure of phase 1

Specific principles and suggested structure	
The assessment of teacher achievement results in a credit rating of 40 M-level credits (in some cases derived in part from a carrying forward of 30 credits from previous M-level work)	
Module 1 (30 credits)	**Either** a. 30 carry-forward credits, where you can demonstrate through use of skills of enquiry and use of evidence that there has been previous impact of your practice on children's and young people's outcomes PLUS Module 2a *OR* b. Work within the four content areas which develop your skills of enquiry and the use of evidence, in relation to the impact of your practice on the outcomes of children and young people PLUS Module 2b
Module 2 (10 credits)	**Either** a. Work that focuses on using and further developing these M-level skills in researching the impact of your practice on children's and young people's outcomes in your new practice *OR* b. A research activity that further develops M-level skills of enquiry into the impact of your practice on children's and young people's outcomes in your new practice
For all NQTs there will be a personalised programme that complements the learning opportunities provided by local authorities and schools as part of their induction programme.	
Phase 1 Learning outcomes	
By the end of phase 1, the teachers on the MTL programme demonstrate that they have developed their professional attributes, knowledge, skills and understanding in their practice so that teaching is effective and there is increasingly positive impact on the outcomes of the children and young people they teach. This will require the teacher to: ● identify personalised professional learning needs in their new context; ● draw on and critique a knowledge base, related to the four content areas of MTL; ● undertake a critical and enquiry-based approach to their professional practice so that it continuously impacts effectively on the outcomes for children and young people	

If you do not have previous master's-level credits, your coach and tutor will together help you to plan a way in which you can *develop your skills of enquiry and the use of evidence, in relation to the impact of your practice on the outcomes of children and young people.* As in the case of those who already have 30 credits, the further 10 credits may be achieved by using your work during induction.

In both cases, you will need to keep a well-structured portfolio of your induction work to use as appropriate in phase 1. During your NQT year, you will be supported by mentors and coaches in your school, as you work through the three CEDP transition points, and through these, reflect on what you have done and learned, and identify your further learning needs.

At each stage, there is an opportunity for you to personalise your forward planning to take account of your professional development needs. The four content areas of the MTL (discussed in more detail in each of Chapters 3, 4, 5 and 6) provide a helpful framework of prompts to assist you in this.

Although you should have completed transition point 1 at the end of your ITT period, you may reflect on this as you prepare, at the start of your first post, to complete transition point 2. Your induction tutor and/or school-based coach will help you review your ITT period, and discuss your development priorities. This is an important process, as they may have changed, depending on the context of your new workplace. Your HEI tutor may also be involved at this stage, assisting you in negotiating a way to present the report of your activities for assessment purposes. During this period, you will find many helpful materials and outline proformas on the TDA website (**www.tda.gov.uk**) and you will see that your priorities should very naturally link to the four MTL content areas, and that they will, in fact, provide a helpful focus.

In 2008, the DCSF published its *Statutory Guidance on Induction for Newly Qualified Teachers in England* (2008c), indicating that induction programmes should:

> *assist the NQT to meet the core standards by the end of the period and equip him or her with the tools to be an effective and successful teacher. Each NQT's programme should be tailored to the individual's needs and circumstances and should provide a reduced timetable (and planning, preparation and assessment time) and significant opportunities for the NQT to:*
> * *show their potential;*
> * *make rapid advancement towards excellence in teaching; and*
> * *begin to make a real impact on their school's and pupils' development.*

Phase 1 of the MTL, in linking specifically to the CEDP transition points, formalises both this process and the academic recognition of it. During this phase, you will also be working towards achieving the core standards (having successfully achieved the QTS standards in your ITT). Your MTL work can help provide evidence for your mentor that you have achieved the standards, and conversely, working towards the standards can help focus your MTL work.

Reflection

It is likely that you will keep a portfolio of your evidence during this NQT year. Explore the suggested frameworks available on the TDA website, and the resources and guidance. Using these (or any other ideas that you might have), consider how they will suit both your needs, and the needs of the MTL. Discuss with colleagues on the MTL, mentors and coaches, and your HEI tutor how best you might begin to keep your portfolio. Discuss with your tutor the requirements and criteria for assessing phase 1.

Preparing for the next phase: assessment and progression through the MTL

At this initial stage of your MTL, you will be starting to develop the skills of reflection to a much greater extent than before, and using this to help you assess the impact of your practice on your pupils, and to help you plan to improve it. While initially, you will probably work on developing the knowledge and practical skills of teaching, as you progress, you should be able to also understand, in a deeper and more critical way, the concept of being a reflective and responsive practitioner. This concept will be explored later in this chapter, but it is worth first of all looking at how this deeper-level understanding relates to both progression through an aspect of professional standards and also to the master's-level benchmark statements, since both of these will form an integral part of your MTL experience and its assessment. Table 2.2 shows the progression from QTS to Advanced Skills teacher for one of the professional standards.

You will notice that initially, you progress to a higher level standard by having a broader knowledge base, but in the move to excellent teacher, a much more critical understanding of teaching and learning issues is the key indicator. Undertaking postgraduate study as part of your ongoing professional development allows you to address this aspect of your practice, and in doing so can help support your career development.

Action Point

Discuss with your school-based coach how you might move towards C10 from Q10, and perhaps to P2. Plan the activities that you could do in order to help you make this progression. Consider and discuss how you might present the evidence to support a claim that you have progressed.

Learning and assessment opportunities

Your HEI tutor, supported by your school-based coach, has responsibility to ensure that learning and assessment opportunities are appropriate. The TDA identifies the key features of assessment, outlining that teachers will be assessed:

- *against the MTL learning outcomes, for each phase, based on an integration of the Professional Standards for Teachers and the QAA M-level benchmarks;*
- *in ways that are personalised, with the teacher, coach and tutor needing to decide which forms of assessment are most suited to meeting the needs of the teacher, while providing secure evidence of achievement of standards and benchmarks;*

Table 2.2 Progression from QTS to Advanced Skills teacher

Professional Standard		Professional Knowledge and Understanding requirement	M-Level Standard
QTS Q10		Have a knowledge and understanding of a range of teaching, learning and behaviour management strategies and know how to use and adapt them, including how to personalise learning and provide opportunities for all learners to achieve their potential	A systematic understanding of knowledge, and a critical awareness of current problems and/ or new insights, much of which is at, or informed by, the forefront of their academic discipline, field of study, or area of professional practice
Core C10		Have a good, up-to-date working knowledge and understanding of a range of teaching, learning and behaviour management strategies and know how to use and adapt them, including how to personalise learning to provide opportunities for all learners to achieve their potential	
Post-threshold P2		Have an extensive knowledge and understanding of how to use and adapt a range of teaching, learning and behaviour management strategies, including how to personalise learning to provide opportunities for all learners to achieve their potential	
Excellent E3		Have a critical understanding of the most effective teaching, learning and behaviour management strategies, including how to select and use approaches that personalise learning to provide opportunities for all learners to achieve their potential	
Advanced Skills		No additional specification at this stage	

- in ways that are flexible, with the teacher, coach and tutor deciding when the teacher is ready to present evidence for assessment purposes, and which forms of assessments will be used as being most fit for purpose;
- in ways that reflect the practice-based nature of the MTL, with the teacher demonstrating their professional learning;
- in ways that take full account of the other demands on the teacher's time, with the coach and tutor matching the timing and forms of assessment to the teacher's professional responsibilities in the school and to her/his personal life. The coach and

tutor must ensure that the MTL does not in any way undermine the work/life balance that each teacher is expected to be able to achieve.

(The National Framework for Masters in Teaching and Learning, TDA, 2009)

From this you can expect to find a range of assessment tasks that may differ to ones you have encountered during your ITT and other educational experiences.

While guidance on assessment will be given by both your tutor and school-based coach or mentor on each specific assessment task, you will find that there will be a range of formats of assessment which will reflect the practice-based nature of the programme. You will have opportunities to discuss and indeed negotiate these assessments with your tutor and coach or mentor. You will also be given some advice in this and subsequent chapters about the academic skills required. Karen Castle's (2009) text *Study Skills for your Masters in Teaching and Learning* provides further guidance, and is a useful companion to this text.

Let us now explore some of the assessment requirements in more depth. The remaining part of this chapter is devoted to providing you with some reference materials to support you as you prepare to progress, and that you can also revisit as you move through the other two phases. It is likely that your experience will be structured to give you assessment opportunities such as:

- annotated presentation;
- critical incident analysis;
- learning log and critical reflection;
- case study of a child, class or school-based or wider issue (you will be encouraged to explore content areas within each of these contexts during your MTL);
- practitioner research, including action research;
- production of artefact with supplementary reflection;
- annotated bibliography.

Ideally, you should undertake a number of different assessment formats, and your coach and tutor will help you negotiate those best suited to your own personal and professional needs at each stage of your MTL. You will see however, that while the formats you choose may be different in their presentational requirements, they all share a common feature in asking you to display key skills of working at master's level. Specifically, this requires you to demonstrate that you can:

- critically reflect on practice and learn from the analysis of these reflections;
- engage in enquiry and research into practice, report findings, and through analysis, make sound judgements;
- engage critically with academic reading;
- act ethically;
- articulate your learning in an appropriate manner at an appropriate level.

Let us now explore each of these in turn. Under each heading, the main features and skills will be explained, and a range of other readings referred to. At the end of each, there will be reflections and action points.

Critical thinking and reflective practice

Critical thinking

This is a skill which is important throughout your MTL study, and one which is worth while considering in some detail. To quote an Open University Study guide, *Acquiring critical thinking skills helps you to develop more reasoned arguments and draw out the inferences that you need to use in your assignments, projects and examination questions* (**www.open. ac.uk/skillsforstudy/critical-thinking.php**). You will probably be able to find many texts about it, and many definitions of it. Definitions will all, however, centre around the processes of reasoned and disciplined thinking, in order to make justifiable and sound judgements in a given situation. Many texts will break this down into a staged process as outlined below.

1. Process
2. Understand
3. Analyse
4. Compare
5. Synthesise
6. Evaluate
7. Apply
8. Justify

Not all the work you do towards your assessments will require you to go through all these stages, but you will see that as you begin to evaluate your own teaching and conduct enquiry, that you will increasingly need the later stages of this process.

There are some guiding principles which can help you develop your capacity for and skill in critical thinking. Hughes (2000) suggests that each sound argument is characterised by three criteria.

1. *The premise(s) of the argument must be acceptable.*
2. *The premise(s) of the argument must be relevant to the conclusion.*
3. *The premise(s) of the argument must provide adequate support for the conclusion.*

(Hughes, 2000, pp115–16)

These are important criteria to bear in mind when you are constructing an argument or position, at the end of a period of reading, reflection or evaluation of evidence in an enquiry. It can be very easy to be sidetracked when dealing with complex issues, and lose sight of the relationship between the premises of any argument, and the conclusion reached. Likewise, relevancy can also be overlooked, especially when you have a strong emotional response to what you have read or what you have found.

You may also be in a position where you need to assess the strength of some research findings for example, or how to assess the soundness of the conclusions drawn in an article you are reading, and again, Hughes provides some useful staged guidelines.

1. Identify the main conclusion
2. Identify the premises
3. Identify the structure of the argument
4. Check the acceptability of the premises
5. Check the relevance of the premises
6. Check the adequacy of the premises
7. Look for counter-arguments

These are useful self-checking mechanisms also, which will help you ensure that any work you do for your MTL assessments is based on sound and logical principles.

If you cannot access the Hughes text, you will find many others available in libraries. Your HEI will almost certainly give you access to electronic resources, which you will be able to access from your own workplace or home. HEIs like the Open University also publish on open websites many study aids and guides. Their critical thinking support can be found at **www.open.ac.uk/skillsforstudy/critical-thinking.php**

You may also find Jenny Moon's (2008) book, *Critical Thinking: An exploration of theory and practice*, a useful and accessible read in helping develop your own critical thinking skills.

Reflective practice

Coupled with critical thinking skills, this is perhaps the foundation stone of your learning in a professional development master's course.

The terms 'reflective practice' and 'critical reflection' will be familiar to you, as something you have been encouraged to do throughout your initial training, and again, as you are completing your NQT year. One of the difficulties of the term 'reflective practice' is that it is almost presumed that everyone understands what it is, and contemporary texts and articles tend to talk more about how useful it is, rather than what it is. In this respect, some of the earlier texts may be a good place to start finding out more about it. The writing of Donald Schön provides the basis of much contemporary thinking around reflective practice. His position was that teachers are skilled in what he calls 'reflection-in-action', that is the thinking that we do on our feet, as and when we are teaching. It relates to the responses we make *in situ* to changing events as they unfold around us. It is triggered by our experiencing something unexpected and responding to that. We draw on previous knowledge and experience in order to help us respond. You may have noticed how well developed this capacity is in experienced teachers.

> *The practitioner allows himself to experience surprise, puzzlement, or confusion in a situation which he finds uncertain or unique. He reflects on the phenomenon before him, and on the prior understandings which have been implicit in his behaviour. He carries out an experiment which serves to generate both a new understanding of the phenomenon and a change in the situation.*
>
> (Schön, 1983, p68)

The 'experiment' that Schön refers to here is the way in which a teacher tries out something different, when a planned approach seems to need revision.

Schön also talks of 'reflection-on-action', distinguishing this from 'reflection-in-action' in that it occurs after an event. The practitioner may write a report of an event, or have a discussion with a mentor or colleague and use this as the focus of deliberative reflection.

Smith (2001) suggests that:

> *The act of reflecting-on-action enables us to spend time exploring why we acted as we did, what was happening in a group and so on. In so doing we develop sets of questions and ideas about our activities and practice.*
>
> *The notion of repertoire is a key aspect of this approach. Practitioners build up a collection of images, ideas, examples and actions that they can draw upon. Donald Schön, like John Dewey (1933: 123), saw this as central to reflective thought.*
>
> (Smith, 2001)

This notion of repertoire is highly significant as you develop as a teacher. The acts of reflecting in and on action allow you to build up a repertoire of images and understandings of your practice which allow the formulation of 'wise judgement' in your professional life. It is this type of reflection that you normally engage in when you have to write a reflective account of your learning after something you have done.

The full text of the paper presented by Schön in 1987 to the American Educational Research Association makes a very readable explication of his ideas of reflective practice. It is available at **http://educ.queensu.ca/~russellt/howteach/schon87.htm** and I think it will challenge you to reconceptualise your own notion of reflection, and research. I would urge you to read this, discussing it with your mentor or coach, peers and tutor as you progress through your MTL.

Much contemporary writing conceptualises reflective practice as a process where thought and action are inseparable (see Osterman and Kottkamp, 2004, for example). Texts such as this focus on the concept of double-loop learning. Double-loop learning is seen as a more holistic notion of learning than the more familiar, single-loop, Kolb cycle, in that the activity is seen as part of a larger cycle, in which the reflection takes place on the fact of engaging in the activity and the assumptions implicit in it.

Usher and Bryant (1989) describe this as follows:

Double-loop learning...'involves questioning the role of the framing and learning systems which underlie actual goals and strategies'.

(Usher and Bryant, 1989, p87)

Brookfield (1995) discusses the rift between our intentions and the outcomes of them and suggests critical reflection as a means by which we can ameliorate the feelings of self-doubt and guilt that such a situation can precipitate. He suggests that we are all susceptible to assumptions, paradigmatic, prescriptive and causal.

Paradigmatic assumptions are, he suggests, the hardest for us to challenge, as they represent the way in which we have learned to see and understand the world. Most of us are highly resistant to such challenges, as we recognise that if changes occur, the consequences may be explosive.

Prescriptive assumptions are rooted in what we think will happen in particular situations. Do we assume for example that students in A-level classes will be self-directed learners because they have voluntarily chosen to study a particular subject? Do we structure our teaching around this assumption?

Causal assumptions are almost part and parcel of the everyday practice of teachers. Indeed, interventionist policy is predicated on the concept of 'if we do action x, then outcome y will improve'.

Brookfield asserts that identifying (which may be much more difficult that we realise – and the self-checking mechanism of assessing the strength of an argument (Hughes, 2000) may be a useful way in which to do this) and challenging our assumptions is the essence of critical reflection. He gives some excellent, and highly relevant examples of this in Chapter 1 of his book, *Becoming a Critically Reflective Teacher*. Reading this book will challenge many of your own assumptions, not least of all about what constitutes reflective practice.

A key tool in the repertoire of the reflective practitioner is the journal or diary. Kemmis and McTaggart (1981) suggest using a diary to record reactions to events, reflections on them, tentative interpretations of them, and to construct provisional hypotheses. Moon (2006, p1) claims that the learning journal is essentially a *vehicle for reflection*. She claims that 6 key things occur in writing a learning journal:

- *Journals slow the pace of learning*
- *Journals increase the sense of ownership of learning*
- *Journals acknowledge the role of emotion in learning*
- *Journals give learners an experience of dealing with ill-structured material*
- *Journals encourage metacognition (learning about one's own process of learning)*
- *Journals encourage learning through the process of writing*

(Moon, 2006, pp26–36)

You can see an excellent example of how Jane, a student on a professional development master's programme, used her learning journal and those of her students to enhance the learning in their classroom, in Chapter 3. She uses diaries to enhance her critical thinking about practice, moving 'normal' reflections from the more pragmatic to a more critically reflective basis, and thus helping her to understand the relationship between theory and practice. At their best, diaries or journals become a place where you can start to theorise your own practice:

> …the theoretical necessity of a reflexive conception of research's relation to action, so that their relationship may be theorised in ways which preserve the authenticity of both, i.e. which preserves research's capacity for achieving a critical distance from action, AND preserves action's intelligibility, as a creative, rather than a causally determined response to interpretive meaning.
>
> (Winter, 1987, p22)

This, and revisiting Brookfield's notion of challenging assumptions, leads smoothly to the concept of educational enquiry and practitioner research.

Action Point

Produce an outline of your own understanding of reflective practice. You can do this in bullet points, or in diagrammatic form if you prefer. The important thing is that you start to clarify in your own mind what might be required of you when you are asked to produce a reflective account of some aspect of your practice or learning. Then read Chapter 1 of Brookfield's book, and assess your own notes or diagram against his ideas. Do you feel that you need to revise anything in your understanding? Discuss this with peers, your coach and your tutor.

Educational enquiry and practitioner research

Much of the assessment work you do will be completed through some form of enquiry or practitioner research. Your assignments will focus on your explorations of your developing practice as a teacher. If we consider the notions of critical thinking coupled with reflective practice, you will see that you are beginning to have the skills to extend this into a more formalised enquiry into your practice. If you have read the texts suggested earlier, you will have seen a close link between reflection and practice development. Educational enquiry extends the notion of reflective practice to enable you to take into consideration a wider range of views and feedback on your teaching experiences. On the whole, however, enquiry starts with something that you notice and reflect on. As Mason (2002) notes in the preface to his excellent book, *Researching Your Own Practice: The Discipline of Noticing*:

> As a professional, you are sensitised to notice certain things in professional situations. To develop your practice means to increase the range and decrease the grain size of

relevant things you notice, all in order to make informed choices as to how to act in the moment, how to respond to situations as they arise.

(Mason, 2002)

This has resonances with Schön's concept of reflection-in-action, and is the basis of much educational enquiry. However, moving from a self-reflective practitioner to an enquiring one, and then to practitioner–researcher requires both a broadening of scope and a systematisation of approach. Chapter 9 of Mason's book is very helpful in outlining the key features of research, and thus, showing you how you can move to this position in your own professional development work.

In order to turn from personal professional development to research, you have to address the question of convincing others of what you claim to have found out.

(Mason, 2002, p176)

He also very usefully outlines and describes different ontologies, that is, different ways in which to view the world. He relates these clearly to the types of studies which reside within them. This is an essential consideration in any type of research, as the approach you use to conduct the research must be appropriate, and philosophically suited to the research question or focus.

One of the key features of practitioner (or indeed any form of) research is the use of data. Your own reflective journal or diary will provide a rich source of such data. However, you will realise that it is an incomplete representation of what has been happening. We are all familiar with 'asking to hear the other side' of any situation, and quickly come to realise that without, for example, asking for a range of views and perspectives, we do not fully understand what has happened, and as such, are not in a position to make judgements. A range of data sources is readily available to you as a practitioner–researcher. In any classroom situation for example, you can readily elicit your own views, and the views of the students, and perhaps with not too much extra effort, the views of another professional such as a teaching assistant or colleague willing to act as a critical friend. Interviews, questionnaires, and focus groups are all well-recognised ways of collecting the views and perceptions of others, and if semi-structured, rather than tightly structured and closed, allow you to probe deeper into what they are saying, and what it might mean.

You will also have access to a broad range of other data on student performance and attainment, behaviour and attendance. Added to these primary data sources is a range of documents relating to your practice: curriculum documents, school policy documents, minutes of meetings all form a useful backdrop to help your understanding of what is happening. Chapter 7 of this book will discuss concepts of data in a little more detail, and also discuss the way in which you can turn this naturally occurring data into evidence to support any claims you make.

In the meantime however, you may want to start familiarising yourself with some common approaches to educational enquiry and research.

One particular and powerful research approach for educationalists is one which you may already be familiar with, action research. In many ways, this is the perfect practitioner development approach as it is both research and practice development and has as its starting point critical reflection on your own practice.

> *However, although the possibility of change is grounded in the distinction between action and research, it requires equally an intimate and principled linkage between the two, in order that the 'findings' of research can be translatable back into the world of action.*

(Winter, 1987, p21)

Action research has been variously defined and described, but a useful starting point is the definition given by Elliott (1991, p49): *the fundamental aim of action research is to improve practice rather than to produce knowledge.* This immediately taps into the agenda of the practice-based MTL. You can find many excellent texts and web-based resources to support your engagement with this type of practitioner research. In particular, although written for associate/part-time tutors in higher education, the Open University Action Research Guide (available at **www.open.ac.uk/cobe/docs/AR-Guide-final.pdf**) is a clear and detailed 'walk-through' the practical and thought processes of engaging in action research. Likewise, Water-Adams provides an excellent resource at **www.edu.plymouth.ac.uk/resined/actionresearch/arhome.htm**. The Alberta Teachers' Action Research Guide is detailed and easy to follow for the novice action researcher, and is available at **www.teachers.ab.ca/SiteCollectionDocuments/ATA/Quick%20Links/Publications/.pdf**

You will notice that however represented, all action research models share a common format of cyclicality, the cycle being represented at its simplest as repeated series of reflect, plan, act, and observe activities (see Figure 2.1).

Initial reflection comes from some initial concern or question which arises in your practice, and your desire to find out more about what is happening, in order to develop customised approaches to resolving the concern. Elliott (1991, p71) presents a more detailed diagrammatic representation of each cycle.

Other research approaches which are commonly used are based on case study methodologies, where you can undertake an evaluative, exploratory, explanatory, illustrating, theory testing, or theory generating study into practice. It is unusual to undertake experimental type studies in practitioner research, as there are firstly major ethical issues involved in this, and secondly, there is also an issue of proving causality in the field of complex human behaviour.

Case studies share a number of key features.

- *The focus is on a contemporary phenomenon in a real-life context.*
- *The researcher has little control over events.*
- *They ask 'How' and 'Why' questions.*
- *They can use a range of data types, qualitative and quantitative.*

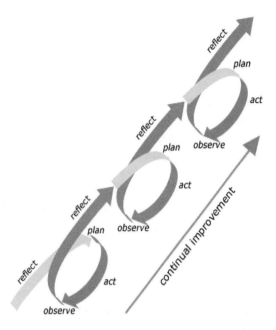

Figure 2.1 *Action research cycles*

- *They focus upon particular individual actors or groups of actors and their perceptions.*
- *They feature rich, vivid description of events within the case.*
- *They study both the particularity and the complexity of the case.*

(Stake, 1995)

As Bassey (1999, p62) suggests, *The singularity [of the case] is chosen because it is expected in some way to be typical of something more general. The focus is the issue rather than the case itself.*

Whichever approach you choose to take in your own research, and whatever methods you choose to use for data collection, depend primarily on the type of question you choose as your focus, and it is crucial that you are able to defend this choice both academically, and in terms of fitness for purpose.

You will also need to be able to demonstrate that your research is rigorous and valid. There are many mechanisms for ensuring that your research is 'good quality'. You are probably familiar with the concept of replicability in scientific research: *if you do it exactly as the method says, you too will get results like this.* This is the basis of many of our everyday activities from taking painkillers for a headache, to baking cakes. Both depend on the notion that the approach has been tried and tested in a range of randomised situations, and has been found to be both replicable and reliable. However, in the complex world of human behaviour, this degree of replicability is not achievable. How often have you seen one group of pupils respond very positively to a particular type of teaching, while another group has a strong negative response? Indeed, the positive response group may later respond nega-tively, depending on what their last lesson was, what they had for lunch, whether it is windy outside – this list is endless. What is clear from this is that human behaviour is not very predictable, and a particular method which works in one particular situation may not be replicable in another situation. For this reason, writers suggest different indicators of quality may be more appropriate in practitioner educational research. Qualities such as authenticity, truthfulness, applicability, credibility, dependability, transferability are all used in the context of the more naturalistic research that practitioners tend to engage in.

Peter Reason's 2005 paper *Choice And Quality In Action Research Practice* outlines four characteristic dimensions of quality research. (**http://people.bath.ac.uk/mnspwr/Papers/ChoiceandQualityinActionResearchPractice.pdf**).

Reflection

Reflecting back on action research and case study approaches, consider a situation in your own practice or context that you think you might wish to research. Discuss the possibility of undertaking enquiry in this area with your coach and tutor, and prepare a brief outline plan. Share this with your colleagues also, and in particular, discuss the possible research approach that would be appropriate.

Academic reading, writing and talking

During your MTL you will be required to read academic literature relating to your studies. There will be a range of reasons for doing this, but a central one will be to develop your own knowledge of your subject and area of study. You will probably at some stage have to complete a systematic literature search and review relating to a particular topic. The purpose of this literature review is to provide an account of what has already been written by scholars and researchers on the topic, and present an analysis of it. In doing this, you need to keep your own research focus to the fore, so that your review is relevant, and read critically in order to find what weakness and strengths exist in existing research findings. Your literature review should demonstrate that you can search for and read literature effectively, and also that you can critically appraise what you have read. At the end of it, you should be able to identify how it relates to and/or guides your own research.

Having collected and collated data, and read the relevant literature, you are then in a position to start writing or preparing your own report. The skills of effective reading and effective writing are closely related and students are often told to read more in order to improve their writing. If you can do these (reading and writing) effectively, then you will also have mastered the art of preparing for oral presentation, which may be a form of assessment available to you in your MTL.

Sometimes however, it is difficult to read in a way that does help your writing and oral presentations. Given that much of the communication of your research findings will be communicated via some writing, it is sometimes helpful to explore more clearly the relationship between good reading and good writing. Poulson and Wallace (2004) explain this in a series of related steps.

As a critical reader of the literature, you:	**As a self-critical writer of the literature, you:**
consider the authors' purpose in writing the account	*state your purpose in what you write to make it clear to your readers*
examine the structure of the account to help you understand how the authors develop their argument	*create a logical structure for your account that assists you with developing your argument, and make it clear to your readers*
seek to identify the main claims the authors make in putting forward their argument	*state your own main claims clearly to help your readers understand your argument*
adopt a sceptical stance towards the authors' claims, checking whether they support convincingly what they assert	*assume that your readers adopt a sceptical stance to your work, so you must convince them by supporting your claims as far as possible*
question whether the authors have sufficient backing for the generalisations they make	*avoid making sweeping generalisations in your writing which you cannot justify to your readers*
check what the authors mean by key terms in the account and whether they use these terms consistently	*define the key terms you employ in your account so that your readers are clear what you mean and use these terms consistently*
consider whether and how any values guiding the authors' work may affect what they claim	*make explicit any values that guide what you write*
distinguish between respecting the authors as people and being sceptical about what they write	*avoid attacking authors as people but be sceptical about what they write*
keep an open mind, retaining a conditional willingness to be convinced	*assume that your readers are open-minded about your work and are willing to be convinced if you can adequately support your claims*
check that everything the authors have written is relevant to their purpose in writing the account and the argument they develop	*sustain your focus throughout your account, and avoid irrelevancies and digressions in what you write*

expect to be given the information that is needed for you to be in a position to check any other literature sources to which the authors refer

ensure that your referencing in the text and the reference list is complete and accurate so that your readers are in a position to check your sources

(Poulson and Wallace, 2004, p7)

In addition to writing effectively and self-critically, you also need to ensure that the structure of your writing or oral presentation is clear and coherent. Different tutors may suggest different structures and sequences for your work, and indeed, there can be no single model appropriate for all types of writing or presentation. However, it is likely that most pieces you write will need to share a common set of characteristics.

- An introduction which introduces the reader or listener to what you are going to do in the assignment, introduces your research aim, question or focus, and gives both a rationale for your choice of focus, and some description of the context in which the research is located.
- Literature review, presented as a critical summary of what is already known in the field, and the preparation for your own research (which could be prompted by gaps in previous research, or a desire to test further).
- Discussion of methodological approach to your research or enquiry, and description of how you will collect and collate data.
- Presentation of your findings with analysis of what they mean. You should develop this section by reference to the theoretical frameworks identified in your literature review. You should also present and discuss any unexpected findings here and discuss their meaning and significance. You will also need to back up your argument with the evidence from your study, and will need to consider, and argue against, alternative counter-arguments.
- Discussion of the implications of your findings, particularly focusing on how they contribute to (your) professional knowledge or practice. Can you make recommendations for further research, or for practice or policy development on the basis of your research?

Action Point

Review a recent presentation you have either been to, or have made yourself. If it was a presentation about some research and findings, evaluate it in terms of the points above. What do you think the strengths of the presentation were? Were there any aspects that could have been better developed?

Acting ethically

Ethical thinking is a central feature of all stages of practitioner enquiry or research. As a starting point, it is useful to take the medical precept, *Primum non nocere*: first, do no harm. This is something that every teacher and other educational practitioner practises. However, that precept raises many questions for the practitioner about what 'harm' might actually be or look like. Almost all texts on educational research will contain a section or even a chapter about ethics in this type of research. You will also find many sources of ethics rules or guidelines to assist you in your research. However, adhering to the rules, generally couched in terms of anonymity, confidentiality and informed consent, may prove much more difficult than at first realised. Much of the work you do for your MTL will be centred around your own practice in your own school. How might anonymity be guaranteed in such circumstances? What does informed consent mean when working with children and vulnerable young people? How can you guarantee no harm to participants?

Pring (2000) differentiates between the rules and principles of ethics. For example, while the rules for driving a car include *Keep to the left hand side of the road* and *Never overtake on a double white line*, these are subordinate to a general principle such as *You ought to drive in such a way as not to cause harm to others*. For example, if driving in the UK, the rule will still be drive on the left, while if driving in France, the rule will be drive on the right. In both cases however, the overarching principle is maintained, that of driving in a way that will not cause harm to others.

Likewise, in your own research contexts, you will need to establish what principles of ethics you will adhere to, and then decide how these can be operationalised for the purpose of your research. This will involve you being able to negotiate procedures within your research. You also need to consider the fact that as research progresses, things will change. New ideas may emerge, or you may realise you need access to different types of information, and as such, the negotiation of ethical procedures is an ongoing process throughout the research. Chapter 3 of Burton and Bartlett's (2009) book *Key Issues for Education Researchers* is an excellent introduction to taking an ethical approach to research.

The British Educational Research Association (BERA) has published a set of guidelines for researchers based on respect for:

- the person;
- knowledge;
- democratic values;
- the quality of educational research;
- academic freedom.

  In conducting educational research, researchers also have a set of responsibilities to:

  - *participants;*
  - *sponsors of the research;*
  - *the community of educational researchers.*

  (BERA, 2004)

While some of the guidelines are not particularly relevant to practitioner and novice researchers, they do form a useful starting point from which to derive your own principles of ethics in your research.

What is clear, once you start reading about ethics in research, is that this is not a 'tick-box' exercise. Ethical soundness is not achieved by simply ticking the anonymity and confidentiality boxes found on many ethics approval forms you may have come across. You need to think about ethical issues from the moment you start considering the focus of your research, through the choices you make about participants, data collection, implications and consequences of your findings, possible changes in policy and/or practice that may result, and at all times, be open to the possibility that you may need to review and revise the way in which you think about these matters.

Action Point

Read Chapter 3 of *Key Issues for Ethical Researchers* (Burton and Bartlett, 2009), and discuss with your coach and tutor how an enquiry in your practice might be ethically designed, carried out, and written up or reported on. What do you think the key ethical issues might be? How might you address them in a meaningful way?

Bringing it all together

Having now explored some of the concepts underpinning the work that you will carry out during your induction year in phase 1, and the processes that will become a central part of all your work in phases 2 and 3, you should begin to have some idea of the range of activities that you will take part in, and the range of ways in which you can provide evidence of your learning. Each of the next four chapters will give some suggestions for assessment tasks which you can discuss with your coach and tutor. Chapter 7 will give further support for undertaking and reporting on research activities, and will discuss in more depth the concept of the use of evidence in your research and practice.

Summary

At the end of this chapter, you should have developed a clear understanding of:
- how the first stage (phase 1) of the MTL will relate to your induction year;
- the academic process of reading, writing and oral presenting that will underpin your work on the MTL;
- critically-reflective practice;
- the concepts of practitioner enquiry and research;
- the nature and significance of ethical issues in educational research.

PART TWO

PHASE 2 – BROADENING AND EMBEDDING

CHAPTER 3

Content area 1: Teaching, learning and assessing

Put simply, personalised learning and teaching means taking a highly structured and responsive approach to each child's and young person's learning, in order that all are able to progress, achieve and participate. It means strengthening the link between learning and teaching by engaging pupils – and their parents – as partners in learning.

(Report of the Teaching and Learning in 2020 Review Group)

Chapter Objectives

The specific chapter objectives are to provide you with:
- **an understanding of theoretical perspectives on teaching and learning;**
- **support for exploring strategies to support teaching and learning;**
- **an understanding of the personalised learning agenda and its practice;**
- **an understanding of the principles and practice of assessment for learning;**
- **an understanding of the relationship between assessment and the planning of effective teaching;**
- **an understanding of a range of forms and mechanisms of assessment.**

Throughout the chapter, you will be challenged to explore and unpick your own assumptions about teaching, learning and assessment.

Links to the professional core standards
This chapter, as you might expect, addresses many of the professional standards. The key ones addressed are listed below.

Professional knowledge and understanding
C10, C11, C12, C13 and C14

Assessment, Monitoring and Giving Feedback
C31, C32, C33 and C34

You will see a table showing how these feed into the higher standards in Appendix 1.

Introduction

This chapter is constructed in two sections. Section 1 will focus on teaching and learning, and will explore ways in which you can develop your own practice as a teacher. In particular, it will focus on meeting the needs of you as a teacher, and the needs of the children you teach. You can find further details of personalised learning on the DCSF standards site.

Section 2 will focus on assessment, and will encourage you to develop your understanding of the term 'assessment for learning', through questioning some assumptions, reflecting on evidence and considering your own practice.

Section 1: Teaching and learning

Introduction

As a newly qualified teacher, you will begin to experience the complexity of the teaching and learning processes, and the relationships between them. When we reflect on our own experiences of having been taught, and having learned effectively, it is sometimes difficult to pinpoint key factors that may have 'worked' at the time. At the third Cambridge Assessment Research Seminar (January 2008) entitled: *What makes a good teacher? An overview of teaching effectiveness research*, keynote speakers Professor Patricia Broadfoot, Professor Mary James and Professor Deborah Myhill all attempted to summarise recent and relevant research, and draw some common principles. All three made reference to the social aspects of learning and the relationships between teachers and learners. In addition, they recognised good subject knowledge, coupled with an understanding of pedagogy as central in good teaching. Deborah Myhill takes this a step further, arguing that while good subject knowledge and intellectual ability were both important, they were not sufficient to produce a good teacher, but needed to be supplemented by the crucial ability to reflect on one's own performance and then to change it. Mary James echoes this, suggesting that teachers should be reflexive and that their own learning should be maintained.

Clearly then, good teaching and learning are not something that can be oversimplified, but are a rich and complex interplay of a range of factors. As a qualified teacher, you will have become familiar with a range of typologies of learning style. The notion that there are individual learning styles emanates from the 1970s, and was developed and popularised through the work of Kolb on experiential learning in the 1980s. Most teachers today are familiar with cognitive theories, social and emotional theories, and sensory theories such as Gardner's multiple intelligences theory, Goleman's emotional intelligence theory, and the neurolinguistic programming derivatives of visual, auditory and kinaesthetic (VAK) classifications, and indeed a range of other typologies. For most teachers, these concepts form a central part of the planning of their teaching.

In this text, I am not going to produce an analysis of any or all of these, but simply want to encourage you, as a developing teacher, to explore them in an informed and questioning way. They should form part of your background reading to support this stage of your professional development, so that you are up to date in your knowledge of the range of teaching and learning theories that might help in developing your practice and your under-standing of it.

In *About Learning*, (2008, p11), the report of the Demos Learning Working Group, the authors caution the reductionist use of many of these approaches however, suggesting that they are often used in a way that constitutes poor professional practice, with teachers labelling children *as having a particular learning style and so...provide materials and sources that are appropriate to that style. Students may then come to internalise this label and think of themselves as a certain type of learner who should concentrate on this diagnosed style. In our view, this is poor professional practice that can damage a student's learning and development.* Further, they caution that much of the learning styles work is poorly supported by evidence, both in terms of their theoretical underpinning, and their efficacy in improving learning.

On the other hand, Dunn and Dunn (1978) claim that students perform better on tests, and have better attitudes when taught in a way compatible with their learning style. As a teacher, you will often come across a range of theoretical perspectives, and have to make professional judgements about them. One way of helping you to do this is to become more systematically and critically reflective in your practice. Not only will this enhance your professional understanding and practice, but it will also form an important backdrop for the assessed work you will do as part of your MTL. This type of informed reflection and professional adjudication in your practice can also help you address the concept of perso-nalisation.

Personalised learning and your MTL

A key feature of content area 1 is the concept of personalised learning. The DCSF illustrates this as shown in Figure 3.1.

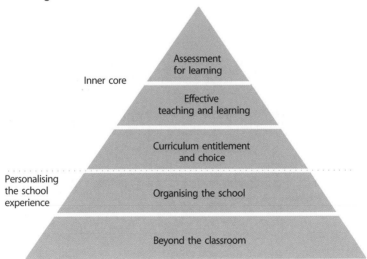

Figure 3.1 Personalised learning

During your early years as a teacher, it is the inner core of this which will be of most immediate concern to you. It is here that your own practice as a classroom teacher is located.

The first two of the elements in Figure 3.1 can provide you with helpful stimuli in terms of choosing the focus of your study for this part of MTL.

You might choose, as Jane did (you will meet Jane later in the chapter), to focus on pedagogy, finding ways in which by working collaboratively, you can devise strategies and pedagogies which are tailored to meet the specific needs of your pupils.

> *Personalised learning demands teaching and learning strategies that develop the competence and confidence of every learner by actively engaging and stretching them.*
>
> *For teachers, it means a focus on their repertoire of teaching skills, their subject specialisms and their management of the learning experience. Personalised learning requires a range of whole-class, group and individual teaching, learning and ICT strategies to transmit knowledge, to instil key learning skills and to accommodate different paces of learning. For pupils, this means a focus on their learning skills and their capability to take forward their own learning.*
>
> **(www.standards.dfes.gov.uk/personalisedlearning/about/)**

The DCSF suggests that personalised learning is enhanced by:

- pupil interviews – all pupils have regular individual, data-informed interviews focusing on their achievement and often involving parents;
- learning from students' views on teaching and learning - pupils' views sought on effectiveness of classroom experience through, for example, surveys and conferences;
- pupil involvement – pupils contributing to whole-school life and to the work of the school;
- being pupil-focused – schools focused around the needs of pupils rather than teachers; students receive consistently good experience of school, pupil inclusion is seen as a guiding principle;
- positive school environment – pupils feel secure and can flourish as individuals; and there are clear sanctions combined with praise where earned for all pupils;
- physical environment – building schools for the future; quality displays to showcase achievement;
- service standards – guaranteed minimum standards: basic level of consistency in the experience of school for every pupil.

Even as a relatively inexperienced classroom teacher, it is possible for you to address the first five of these through classroom-based action research or practitioner research projects. Many teachers at all stages in their careers undertake such work as part of ongoing professional development, and almost all master's programmes in education will have assignments based on this approach. An added bonus of this approach is that it focuses on your own day-to-day work, and as such, is more easily carried out than other types of research.

What does personalised learning mean for you and your pupils?

For pupils, personalised learning is likely to be characterised by your assuming joint responsibility for the design of pupil learning, having their individual needs addressed, knowing how to identify and begin to address their own weaknesses. You will have access to relevant support to enable them to succeed, to develop respect for others, and to build self-esteem and collaboration skills.

For teachers and support staff, personalised learning means that you will develop skills of interpreting pupil data, and use such data to inform your teaching and your pupils' learning. In practical terms this will require you to participate in high-level professional development activities, to network beyond the school, and to use such opportunities to develop a range of appropriate teaching strategies. Collaborative working with other staff, in particular support staff and other adults from outside the school, will be an integral part of this.

Using reflective journals to support personalised teaching and learning

Chapter 2 of this text introduces the use of reflective journals through which you can explore the understanding and practice of your teaching, and then looks at the ways in which this can be usefully enhanced in order to provide you with a sound evidence base which can inform your future planning of teaching and learning. When you first start teaching, and get opportunities to observe other teachers at work, you begin to realise that no two class groups are alike, and indeed, that no two teachers are alike. You may have admired a more experienced teacher who almost intuitively knows how to get the best from their pupils. How does this happen? How does a teacher learn how to respond to the needs of his or her pupils, and devise strategies which best support their learning?

The case study which follows illustrates one teacher's use of reflection and of her master's study to help her develop a personalised learning approach in her classroom. You will notice that Jane not only develops *skills of interpreting pupil data*, but demonstrates her engagement with *high-level professional development activities* through undertaking research into her own practice.

You will also see the involvement of her pupils, who, as suggested by the personalised learning agenda, begin to assume *joint responsibility for the design of their learning, having their individual needs addressed*.

Case Study

Jane's story

*Throughout this case study, Jane's words are **italicised**, without quotation marks, while mine (I was her tutor on her MA programme) are in normal text.*

Jane is in her fourth year of teaching, having trained as a chemistry teacher. However, she is now mainly teaching physics, up to and including A-level. Her current Year 12 class comprises two girls and five boys, and it is with this class that she undertakes her research. She confesses to having been a poor A-level physics student herself, and brings this background to her study. In an effort to improve her physics teaching, she has undertaken various subject-based courses, and although she is now happy and confident about her subject knowledge, she has a specific concern about her teaching: *How can I make sure that my teaching is interesting, relevant and effective for THIS class?*

As well as being a full-time early career teacher, Jane is also completing an MA in education, and has decided to use this project as the focus of her final year dissertation. She elects to do this through the use of a collaborative action research project with her students.

Stop and Read

Why action research?

Action research has been a key mechanism through which teachers and other professionals have addressed concerns about their professional practice since the early 1970s. It has a very specific purpose, enabling professionals to understand their practice better, and use that enhanced understanding in order to effect changes in their practice. As Elliott says, *the fundamental aim of action research is to improve practice* (Elliott, 1993, p49).

Action research is an effort to understand *the social situation in which the participant finds himself* (Elliott, 1978, p355), and is thus located in the teacher's intrinsic rather than the researcher's external concerns. This makes it an ideal means through which to address issues of personalised learning while actually changing your practice as the study progresses. You will, in effect, have evidence of impact built into your project.

Elliott, J. (1991) *Action Research for Educational Change.* Buckingham: Open University Press. Part 1 of this book is subtitled 'Action research and professional learning', and not only introduces the context and concepts of the teacher-as-researcher, but illustrates this process through the use of three case study reports. Chapter 6 provides a useful and practical introduction to the 'doing' of action research and reflective learning. The last part of the book deals with policy contexts, and may not be so directly relatable to the professional development of beginning teachers.

McNiff, J. (2002) *Action Research: Principles and Practice.* Abingdon: Routledge Falmer. The authors introduce this book as an in-service resource for practising teachers. Presented in three parts, it deals with the background to action research, the practicalities of doing action research, and finally a discussion around the issues facing teacher–researchers. This book is a very useful introduction to the concept of practitioner research and encourages a reflective and questioning exploration of professional practice. It is also worth looking for other texts by McNiff.

Mertler, C (2009) *Action Research: Teachers as researchers in the classroom.* Los Angeles, CA; London: Sage. This is a very accessible book, clearly structured to help you cope with the day-to-day issues involved in action research. The issues dealt with, however, relate to a range of formats of practitioner research, and as such provide a useful read for any teacher-researcher.

Jane's reflection on using action research

I decided to undertake the research using an action research approach. Having previously undertaken some action research, I have become quite a convert. Not only is the research very personal, shaped by myself to fit my own personal circumstances, but the impact is upon my own pedagogy and practice. Additionally, changes where necessary can be made immediately. There is no remote application of someone else's ideas as the research is tailored to one's own personal research area. This high degree of personalisation does not mean though, that the research is ad hoc nor that it has no wider relevance.

Action Point

How does Jane start her study?

She starts her project from a relatively broad concern that her teaching practice could be improved to meet the needs of her students better. In addition, there is a need to raise achievement post-16 in her school. She had three key aims in starting this project.

1. To develop pedagogical approaches and make her own physics teaching more effective in terms of student achievement.
2. To provide physics lessons which interest students.
3. To contribute to school improvement through improved pupil performance.

Unsure as to how exactly she might start this research, she begins to keep a reflective diary, and asks her students if they would do the same. The two girls volunteered, but the boys were a little more reluctant, and although willing to give feedback at the end of the lessons, did not keep diaries in a systematic way.

At the start of the school year, I discussed my research project with my AS physics group. I asked the group if they would be willing to help me to undertake my research and I asked for volunteers, making it as clear as possible that this was an entirely voluntary act on their part.

I had decided to start with a journal approach as, although it would be harder to analyse the data collected, for each journal keeper the data would be completely personalised and would not be influenced by leading questions and would allow each person to express themselves fully.

Stop and Read

Why a reflective diary?

The first stage of an action research project is sometimes called the 'reconnaissance' phase. It is a period during which the nature of the initially broad concern is further explored and clarified, so that the research question can become more clearly focused. Like Jane, you might find it hard to have a specific research question or agenda at first, and so the clarifying process will often be best served by the use of a reflective diary or journal. One of the main advantages of using a diary is that it is a repository for all the events, thoughts and feelings about them, and reflections on them that can be collected together for later analysis. I am indebted to Jennifer Moon (2004, p181) for the following analogy. Dumbledore uses his 'pensieve' in much the same way as a researcher's reflective diary when he has too many thoughts and memories crammed into his mind.

> *'[A]t these times,' said Dumbledore, indicating the stone basin, 'I use the pensieve. One simply siphons the excess thoughts from one's mind, pours them into the basin, and examines them at one's leisure. It becomes easier to spot patterns and links, you understand, when they are in this form.'*

(Rowling, 2000, pp518–19)

A reflective diary is a very powerful means of allowing you to spot patterns and links in your practice, and having done so, you can begin to think about the significance of them, and what you then might do to improve your practice.

Mason, J. (2002) *Researching Your Own Practice: The Discipline of Noticing.* Abingdon: RoutledgeFalmer. This book is introduced with the promise of providing practical ways in which teachers can move from *concern about their students and what they are learning, concern about their teaching ... to doing something about it in a practical disciplined manner.*

There is a strong emphasis on systematic and close observation of practice, which is illustrated throughout by short examples, case studies and activities, carefully constructed to both sensitise the reader to the depths and complexities of professional practice.

Moon, J. (2004) *A Handbook of Reflective and Experiential Learning: Theory and practice.* Abingdon: RoutledgeFalmer. This book aims to develop greater understanding and more practical use of reflective and experiential learning as forms of more sophisticated learning. A strength of this book is the range of practical activities designed to encourage critical reflection on practice, and the associated experiential learning.

Jane's reflection on reflective dairies

During the reconnaissance stage of research I had asked pupils to keep a reflective learning journal of their lessons. This is a report of the impact of reflective journal keeping on two girls from my class. The two girls concerned had been predicted AS grades of C (using the ALIS (Advanced Level Information System) grade prediction indicators). During the first term, they indicated that they found the reflective journal useful, and as a teacher, I became aware of their increasing maturity in terms of their thoughtful engagement with their learning.

At the time of their AS module examinations in January, both pupils seemed upset by their perceived poor performance but, when the results were published, they had actually scored very highly, both achieving A grades.

Jane decided at this stage to discuss the usefulness of the diary exercise with her students. She had noticed first of all, that their initial entries all discussed the usefulness of teaching sessions, using phrases such as *this helped* or *helped with my homework* or *made useful notes*. However, as the research progressed, she noticed that their reflections on her lessons changed, and comments such as *I enjoyed the practical* or *I liked going through the calculations* were typical. This interested her, as she felt that there was perhaps a fundamental shift in their perceptions of their learning. She comments:

Rogers (1969, p158) proposes that 'significant learning takes place when the subject matter is perceived by the student as having relevance for his own purpose' i.e. he acknowledges the utility value. However he goes on (1969, p163) to state that 'self initiated learning which involves the whole persona of the learner – feelings as well as intellect – is the most lasting and persuasive ... This is not learning that takes place "only from the neck up". It is a gut level type of learning.' The implication here is that when students are engaged emotionally with the learning then a much deeper learning can take place.

Jane now describes the conversation with the students.

Initially I discussed the learning journals with them and what impact they felt they had made. One girl said she liked the fact that the journal 'allowed her to put down what she was thinking without having to say it out loud', the other 'that if you were frustrated because you didn't get something it allowed you to get it out so you weren't stressed'. They had both been aware of the fact that the journals had been an emotional release after the lesson and this was one of the reasons that they had engaged with keeping the logs. However, they also were aware of how their reflections were beginning to help them understand their own learning: 'it made me realise that I like to see things written down rather than being shown Powerpoints' and 'it helped you to know for other lessons as well'. This was an interesting revelation, as not only was this new understanding of their own learning helping their physics, but it was also being related to their other areas of study as well.

I then asked whether they had enjoyed physics this year. Both replied 'yes' and interestingly one girl went further: she said, "I didn't think I was going to (enjoy physics) ... honestly the only reason I chose physics was because I thought the class was going to be small so I thought I was going to learn something, not because I liked it or anything like that but it has been a lot more enjoyable than I thought it was going to be." When I then discussed the development from utility to emotional engagement from her journal entries, she had not been aware of this change herself. She acknowledged that although physics had been her last choice for A-levels, it was now an area she was considering studying further at university, as she had enjoyed it 'far more than I expected to'.

We went on to look at the issue of the examination, and I asked about their experiences during the examination, afterwards and at the time of results. About the examination, one stated she 'knew how good our answers had to be to get the marks ... how precise' 'the fact that the boys came out saying "this question was so easy ... so good" and I was thinking, I didn't think that . . . I felt the exam paper was more different to the others we had seen . . . it was more theoretical than maths'. From our discussion, it was apparent that during (and immediately after) the examination they were reflecting on what they felt a good answer should be and were measuring their efforts against a (high) standard of expected response. They were aware of the rigour of the marking in terms of specific scientific terminology and were concerned that their answers weren't good enough. To find the boys discussing the 'easiness' of the paper seemed to have highlighted to them the inadequacies of their answers; they hadn't questioned the boys' ability, only their own.

At the time of the results, one girl commented that she thought it was 'a typing error' the other that 'it was such a relief, that it took a lot of pressure off' and they discussed the fact that it made them realise that the boys 'hadn't "got" the paper' i.e. hadn't understood what the paper was looking for, and it was a relief to realise that they were 'right' about it. We discussed the fact that because they were more reflective, during the examination, as with their day-to-day work, they were always looking to improve the standard, and this is why they felt the examination was hard because they knew their work 'wasn't perfect'.

Jane's action point

At the end of the reconnaissance phase of her action research project, Jane shared her thinking and findings with all the members of the class. She hoped that in doing so, they could together analyse the findings and find a way forward that would help the teaching and learning for them all. Interestingly, the five boys then decided to become involved in reflecting on lessons more systematically also, which meant the whole class was more involved. Jane reflects back on this phase, knowing that from this, she will be able to develop her pedagogical approaches and strategies in a way that will meet the needs of her students in a personal and personalised way.

My discussions with the girls have revealed two very mature, introspective, reflective 17-year-olds. They both engaged with the learning journals and acknowledge that this has helped them to both develop reflective skills about how they learn but to them equally important was the issue of emotional involvement. They both felt that the emotional release regarding for example frustration with a difficult topic or enjoyment (when to express enjoyment in a lesson might seem 'geeky') was a very useful tool. They now seem less pressured by their ability to look for improvement in stressful situations.

For my own learning, I have been surprised by the impact of these logs. I had not expected the students to engage so fully with the logs, nor for them to be so revealing in terms of emotional and cognitive development within the subject area. My further research I hope will enable me to focus on areas where I can improve my pedagogy so that improvements in my teaching lead to improvements in their learning.

Analysing the reflective diary

Perhaps now you are beginning to see just how powerful a tool the reflective journal can be. Jane was beginning to get a clearer picture both of her own teaching strategies and approaches (and was wondering if she relied too much on PowerPoint presentations), and also her students' learning styles. Together, they were beginning to realise that knowing themselves as teacher and learners allowed them to have more meaningful, more personalised experiences in their lessons. Paris and Winograd (in Jones and Idol, 1990, p15) feel that the use of learning journals enables students to enhance their learning by becoming aware of their own thinking as they read, write and solve problems and that a great deal of research supports the importance of metacognition in cognitive development and academic learning.

Elliott, J. (1991) *Action Research for Educational Change*. Buckingham: Open University Press.
McNiff, J. (2002) *Action Research: Principles And Practice*. Abingdon: Routledge Falmer. Chapter 6 in each of these books (referenced earlier) provides practical help in terms of data handling, and in particular, Chapter 6 of McNiff is entitled 'Making sense of the data'. This chapter provides a set of guidelines, clearly illustrated by the use of exemplars, to the process of data collection, collation and interpretation.

Section 2: Assessment for learning

Introduction

You may wish to conduct a study into the assessment of pupils' learning in an attempt to improve the ways in which effective assessment can inform teaching and learning.

> *Assessment for Learning (AfL) means using evidence and feedback to identify where pupils are in their learning, what they need to do next and how best to get achieve this. In practice, this means obtaining clear evidence about how to drive up individual attainment; understanding between teachers and pupils on what they need to improve, and agreement on the steps needed to promote sound learning and progress.*
> **(www.standards.dfes.gov.uk/personalisedlearning/about/)**

The increasing prominence of assessment as a fundamental aspect of the teaching and learning processes has recently fuelled a growing body of interest among both teachers and policymakers. This prominence is evident in the wealth of publications produced by commentators on the subject. You can find further details of this on the QCA website and on the DfES standards site.

What is assessment?

The term 'assessment' is used to convey a range of methods used for the evaluation of pupil performance and attainment (Gipps, 1994), and is a process, according to Harlen (1994), which includes gathering, interpreting, recording and using information about a pupil's response to an educational task.

Classroom assessment has a range of purposes, many of which are contradictory. For example, 'traditional' classroom assessments and reporting processes facilitate comparison among pupils and fulfil accountability demands. Gipps (1994), however identifies that assessment can also serve a 'professional' purpose, that is, it can and should support the teaching and learning process:

> *Assessment to support learning, offering detailed feedback to the teacher and pupil, is necessarily different from assessment for monitoring or accountability purposes.*
>
> (Gipps, 1994, p3)

Having begun to consider the term 'assessment', it seems some view it as a means of impacting upon teaching and learning processes, while for others, it is a means of providing information for third parties.

Stop and Read

Developing your understanding of assessment

Gipps identifies that the contrasting perspectives on assessment present teachers with a dilemma. There are demands for example, for testing at national level to afford comparability, and at the same time a need for assessments to: *map more directly on to the processes we wish to develop* (Gipps, 1994, p12).

Assessment for learning

In seeking to clarify what assessment for learning is, Stiggins (2002) informs us that:

> *The crucial distinction is between assessment to determine the status of learning and assessment to promote greater learning.*
>
> (Stiggins, 2000, p5)

Assessment for learning prioritises students' learning and is usually, Black *et al.* (2003) state, informal in nature and embedded in all aspects of teaching and learning.

The QCDA website offers teachers a range of resources related to assessment for learning and, based on the findings of the Assessment Reform Group (1998), identifies that assessment for learning involves using assessment in the classroom to raise pupils' achievement.

This notion is based on the principle that pupils' learning will improve if they understand the aim of their learning, where they are in relation to this aim and how they can achieve the aim.

This is reminiscent of Sadler's (1989) conceptualisation of formative assessment which, he states, is concerned with how judgements about the quality of student responses can be used to shape and improve competence. Formative assessment involves teacher–learner interaction, shifting the emphasis to actively engage pupils in their learning such that:

> *Teacher–learner interaction goes beyond the communication of test results, teacher judgements of progress and the provision of additional instruction, to include a role for the teacher in assisting the pupil to comprehend and engage with new ideas and problems. The process of assessment itself is seen as having an impact on the pupil as well as the product, the result.*
>
> (Torrance and Pryor, 1998, p15)

Stop and Read

Torrance, H. and Pryor, J. (1998) *Investigating Formative Assessment: Teaching and learning in the classroom*. Guildford: Biddles.

> This text uses data from the Teacher Assessment at Key Stage One (TASK) project, to present the reader with an understanding of the link between assessment and learning, through drawing on a range of perspectives.

Neesom, A. (2000) *Report on Teachers' Perception of Formative Assessment*. London: QCA.

> This is a useful document which presents the outcomes of a survey of teachers' perceptions of formative assessment. It provides a useful summary leaflet on assessment for learning and assessment of learning and includes recommendations for further work in the area.

In much literature, assessment for learning is perceived as synonymous with formative assessment (see for example, Weeden *et al.*, 2002) and indeed the current QCDA documentation uses the two interchangeably.

However, before continuing to discuss assessment for learning in further detail, it is important to note that in Black *et al.*'s (2003) conceptualisation that assessment for learning is the purpose, and formative assessment is the process.

By using the two terms interchangeably we are making the assumption that there is little or no place for summative assessment in the learning process. Yet, summative assessment such as 'formal testing', can, Black *et al.* argue (2003), be used to improve learning.

The following questions may aid your thinking about assessment for learning and formative assessment.

- What do you understand by the term 'assessment for learning'?
- When can an assessment activity help learning?

- Are formative assessment and assessment for learning synonymous with each other?
- Can a summative test be used to improve teaching and learning?
- To what extent do you engage the children in your class in the assessment process?

Action Point

The day-to-day assessment in mathematics guidance paper produced to support the renewing of the Primary Framework for mathematics, claims that the term 'assessment for learning' is now in common use and is well understood. To what extent do you agree with this statement?

Provide yourself with a definition for 'assessment for learning'. You might draw on the following to begin to formulate your definition.

- Mind-map of examples from readings and/or practice.
- Discussions with experienced colleagues.
- Observations of colleagues.

Stop and Read

Black, P. and Wiliam, D. (1998) *Inside the Black Box: Raising Standards through Classroom Assessment*. London: King's College.
  This text is concerned with changes in teachers' practice, providing illustrative examples of classroom work. It highlights the theoretical underpinnings of assessment for learning and formative assessment.
Shepard, L. A. (2000) The role of assessment in a learning culture. *Educational Researcher*, 29, (7): 4–14.
  This article is useful in identifying the links between learning theory and classroom assessment.

Case Study

Amanda and Bethany's story of assessment for learning in practice
In order to improve learning through assessment, Black and Wiliam (1998) established that teachers need to:

- share learning intentions with children;
- involve pupils in self-evaluation;

- provide feedback which leads pupils to recognise the next steps, and how to take them;
- be confident that every pupil can improve and consider pupil self-esteem.

The following section will consider each of these and provide examples from a case study designed to unravel the practice of two experienced teachers in relation to Assessment for Learning. Italics are used to show quotations from the study.

Amanda and Bethany are two experienced Year 6 teachers who agreed for me (Lisa) to observe and discuss their practice with them and their pupils in order that I may have a clearer understanding of how two experienced practitioners engage with assessment for learning.

The following uses extracts from my study to illuminate the characteristics of assessment for learning as identified by the QCDA.

How do Amanda and Bethany share learning intentions with children?

Through observing Amanda and Bethany, it became evident that these two experienced practitioners:

- make explicit reference to the learning objectives;
- provide models.

Make explicit reference to the learning objectives and success criteria

Amanda and Bethany both make explicit references to learning objectives. The following provides some examples of strategies they employ and why.

One key technique employed by both teachers is to make explicit reference to the learning objectives at the beginning of shared work. Each teacher has the objectives for the lesson written on a whiteboard for the pupils to read and then shares these orally with the class:

> *She made the objective of the day's session clear to the children, 'to read aloud with expression'.*

> (Observation 3 of Amanda)

The rationale for this was made clear by each teacher, for example, Amanda stated:

> *I always try to make it clear to the children what they are doing. I start each lesson with a description of the learning objectives and explain to the children what this means to them. I think this is so important as it lets them know exactly what they have got to do and how they can get there.*

> (Amanda)

In addition to sharing objectives with the whole class, both teachers recap on learning objectives before children commence independent work and then repeat this with the group that they are working with. For example:

> *Following the main activity, Bethany reminded the children of the main teaching points and objectives and directed them to work in their groups on an independent writing task...A group of children worked with Bethany. She explained the purpose and recapped on learning objectives.*
>
> (Observation 6 of Bethany)

A further technique that Amanda and Bethany use during group and independent work is to encourage pupils to write down the lesson objective.

For Bethany, this is managed through the title of the work. For example, Nigel's work, dated Wednesday 15 November is titled 'Directed and reported speech'. This title was directly related to the learning objective for the session. Amanda either writes the explicit purpose on the board and the children copy this out at the beginning of their written piece, or she asks the children to devise their own 'purpose' in relation to the particular learning objective. For example, Julie's work, dated 12 June is titled 'A 5 day visit to Dukes House Wood with Year 5/6' and underneath the title Julie has written: *Purpose: The purpose of this report is to report to Mr Kerr, because he wants to find out about the trip to Dukes House Wood.* Susan's purpose is: *To tell the teachers who came to Dukes House Wood how good I think it was.* These 'purposes' link with the objective of the lesson.

But how do the children feel about such strategies?

> *It's good if I know the criteria...it's good if you know what to base your work on.*
>
> (Barry, Amanda's class)

> *When the teacher talks with us it's good, because you hear what it is, sometimes she'll talk and it might get written down, people like to get information in different ways...Miss A does lots of things in the lesson to make sure we all know what we're doing and to help us all.*
>
> (Frances, Amanda's class)

It seems therefore, that for Amanda and Bethany, the sharing of learning objectives is a key feature of their practice.

However, in addition to this, both teachers provide children with models in order to make learning objectives and success criteria explicit.

Provide models

Amanda and Bethany use this technique during shared work at the beginning of lessons. For example:

The teacher then told the class that she would be reading a piece of text, as a model example, and she wanted them to identify the genre.

The children then looked at the persuasive piece and recount to draw out how the author had cleverly misled the reader through choice of vocabulary and illustrations.

(Observation 7 of Amanda)

They also use modelling as a strategy in group work, for example:

Working with a small group of children, the teacher wrote some sentences on the whiteboard. For example: 'I was very disappointed by the quality of the rides at the fairground. Your advertisements showed high quality rides, but on arrival most of the rides were closed or broken. I was very disappointed...' She then asked the children to use the example as a model and suggest new sentences themselves. They gave a selection of sentences orally and the teacher scribed them on the whiteboard.

(Observation 5 of Bethany)

Evidence from the pupil interviews suggests that this is a feature of most of their lessons. For example:

Before we go and do our work, she (Bethany) will do it with us at the beginning of literacy.... When it comes to the end, you know what you've done.

(Michelle, Bethany's class)

The rationale for providing models is explained by each teacher:

Modelling is very valuable, they can relate to it, it's personal to them and they can see why something is good. They can see how their work can be so much better. If it's not their work, if I've started a piece of writing, they can still help to improve it. They might not come up with the original idea, but they can give some input and this gives them a feeling of ownership, even if they have just thought of a good adjective, they have contributed. It usually happens in writing and I do it in most lessons.'

(Bethany)

Amanda also values this technique, claiming that:

It's important that they are given a model or example...I use modelling a lot. It is useful for all abilities and they can see where they need to go to improve their own work.

(Amanda)

Amanda and Bethany also use children's work as a model, typically at the beginning of a lesson, and other children in the class then take ideas forward into their own work, for example:

> *The teacher said that she wanted the class to continue writing their persuasive pieces for the lesson today during group work, but before going to do this she said that she wanted Barry and Julie to read some of the arguments that they had managed to start the previous day. The teacher said that she was pleased with their work, and wanted them to share this with the class. She highlighted that they had been successful in meeting the learning objectives yesterday and that the class were to listen and find out why.*
>
> (Observation 4 of Amanda)

The strategy is also used at the end of a lesson to highlight how the objectives had been met, for example:

> *In the plenary, Bethany explained to the children that she was very pleased with their work and that the learning objective had been achieved by all and to a high standard…Children from the independent group read their poem. Bethany explained how they had met the learning objective to class and how they had been successful.*
>
> (Observation of Bethany)

Reflecting on Amanda and Bethany's strategies

The sharing of learning objectives is perceived by many researchers as being a powerful means of motivating children to learn as it ensures that they are task orientated and have ownership of their own learning. For example, Clarke (1998) states that through shared knowledge, pupil autonomy will develop:

> *The sharing of the learning intention enables the child to know the purpose of the activity, thus transferring much of the responsibility for the learning from the teacher to the child.*
>
> (Clarke, 1998, p8)

Reflection

Now that you have seen how Amanda and Bethany share learning objectives and success criteria with children, it is useful to consider your own practice.

- Do you share learning objectives and success criteria with children?
- If so, how valuable do you find it?
- Do you know how the children feel about your strategies?

Action Point

Reflect on the strategies that you employ as a teacher to share learning objectives and success criteria with children. You may find it useful to maintain a reflective diary as outlined in Chapter 2 to begin to build up evidence of how you engage with pupils.

You may also find it useful to observe an experienced colleague and note the range of strategies that he/she employs.

After a period of several weeks, you will be able to build up a range of evidence (this may include observations, samples of pupils' work, lesson plans, etc.) to illustrate how you engage with children, and can use this to draw up an action plan that is personal to you and your pupils, to develop your skills in sharing objectives and success criteria with children.

How do Amanda and Bethany involve pupils in self-evaluation?

The notion of pupil self-evaluation is perceived as a crucial characteristic of assessment for learning (see for example, Black and Wiliam, 1998; Clarke, 2001).

Amanda and Bethany value the use of pupils identifying their own errors and making suggestions regarding improvement and they use three main techniques for this: pupils working collaboratively, peer evaluation and self-evaluation.

Although the categories of 'pupils working collaboratively' and 'peer evaluation' have similar features, in that pupils are not working independently, they have been identified separately because of the difference in their nature. When pupils are working collaboratively, this implies they are working on the same activity and scaffolding each other's learning in a mutually beneficial manner. It is formative in nature because of the critical discussions that take place to improve work, and 'self-evaluative' because it is independent of the teacher. Peer evaluation serves a different purpose and can be recognised as pupils evaluating individuals' work.

Peer collaboration is generally organised by the class teachers, Amanda and Bethany, who encourage pupils to work together in pairs. This occurs during whole-class, independent and guided work, for example:

Children shared their ideas and Bethany scribed them on the whiteboard. Following this, the teacher asked the children to look at all the scenarios and in the pairs discuss which was the best.

(Observation 6 of Bethany)

The rationale for peer collaboration is explained by the teachers, and Amanda, for example comments:

I get them to work together, because they feed off each other. Adults do, don't they?

(Amanda)

They also encourage pupils to work in pairs to peer-evaluate.

> *During the whole class part of the lesson the children all had their own work with them. The children were asked to read independently their recent persuasive pieces, and asked to identify whether or not they were writing in first person or not. The teacher asked the children to work in pairs to discuss and evaluate their work.*
>
> (Observation 5 of Amanda)

> *The teacher asked the children to work independently on their letters, using the ideas on the whiteboard for support. She asked them to work with response partners to check each other's work.*
>
> (Observation 5 of Bethany)

The teachers both value peers working collaboratively and in an evaluative capacity and explained the reason for this:

> *This is something I do a lot, especially since the NLS (children sharing work with each other in pairs). It's really valuable. They respond to each other and can show each other the good aspects of their work and improve each other's work. I learn best like that, and try to encourage them to do this.*
>
> (Amanda)

However, each teacher acknowledged that such a strategy needed to be adopted with caution. For example:

> *Pupils working together to talk about their learning is very useful, but it must be done with someone who they can work with. The gaps can be broad and so they need to work with someone of similar ability. It can be a chance for the less able to see a good piece of writing, but they might not want to do it.*
>
> (Bethany)

This cautionary note is particularly important if we reflect on the pupils' perspectives of such techniques.

> *Sharing with a friend can give you a rough idea of what people will think, like other audiences, but there'd have to be a clear purpose, you know, with the learning objectives so clear then your friend can get a good idea for you if it is good or not. You'd have to be good at communicating though and have some connection with each other. You need to trust each other. Sometimes friends mark it right even if it's wrong so you look good to your other friends. I like to know the teacher's going to check it.*
>
> *You can talk about the work, but you might think it's right and your friend might think it's wrong. It causes arguments if you don't agree.*
>
> (Susan, Amanda's class)

It's good if you share your work, like when you are doing stories. Marking cards are useful because they give you some ideas of what to look for. But it's not always good because a friend could show you how to put in an adjective, but your friends could be wrong. A friend might just think he knows it but doesn't really. You don't know whether to believe your friends. It's okay, but only if they don't cheat. They mark you higher and expect you to do it for them and you feel under pressure. The teacher needs to mark them or walk about and talk to you.

(Simon, Bethany's class)

In addition, Amanda and Bethany claim that they encourage individual pupils to self-evaluate; for example, Bethany stated:

It is so valuable to get pupils to suggest ways forward themselves. On an individual level it's really important that they can look at their own work and suggest things themselves.

(Bethany)

What is of particular interest with regard to individual pupil self-evaluation is that the observation data revealed that opportunities for pupils self-evaluating in Amanda and Bethany's classes is rare; indeed most pupil self-evaluation occurs within the context of paired work, through collaboration, be this planned or unplanned. For example:

Independent group worked independently to write a mystery ending, using pre-written beginning and middle...Although this was an independent task, children were seen talking to each other, asking questions of each other and before returning to whole class, had read each other's endings.

(Observation 2 of Amanda)

Reflecting on supporting pupil self-evaluation
Harris and Bell (1994) suggest that self-evaluation is a skill that is paramount in today's climate. The aim of self-evaluation is, they claim, not only to encourage pupils to become independent learners, but also to develop their metacognitive strategies:

Each of us needs to take more and more responsibility for our own learning in a world where the knowledge base is increasing at a phenomenal rate, let alone the techno-logical developments which give us all more access to information and more difficulty in discriminating that which is relevant and useful and that which is garbage!

Harris and Bell (1994, p89)

Clarke also illustrates how pupil self-evaluation impacts upon teachers. She describes how teachers gain a greater insight into children's learning needs and make links with feedback and planning, thus highlighting how valuable self-evaluation can be as an assessment tool, with information being very clearly used to impact on future planning.

Reflection

Now that you have seen the way that Amanda and Bethany involve children in evaluation, and noted that self-evaluation for the pupils in these experienced practitioners' classrooms is frequently in the form of pairs discussing work, it is useful to consider your own practice.

- Do you encourage self-evaluation? Why?
- Do children in your class have opportunities for peer evaluation? Why?
- Could your practice be improved?

Action Point

Although Amanda and Bethany claimed that self-evaluation was common in their class-rooms, independent self-evaluation was noted rarely, indeed most 'self-evaluation' was encountered in paired or group work. Amanda and Bethany both raise a cautionary note with regard to peer collaboration and evaluation. In addition, children in their class voiced some concerns about peer evaluation.

If you already make use of peer evaluation, it may be useful to find out how the children in your class feel about this. Christensen and James (2000) provide a useful text that encourages practitioners to gain access to their pupils' voices through the use of partici-patory activities. Consider how you could access the children's voices about peer evaluation. Devise an action plan for conducting a small-scale study to gain the perspectives of children about this aspect of your practice.

If you do not already use peer evaluation, you may consider employing a particular strategy to begin to engage children in the process. Clarke (2003) provides some useful, practical advice regarding this and you may find it useful to adopt a strategy with a group of children and evaluate their perspectives of it.

How do Amanda and Bethany provide pupils with feedback?

Feedback has long been recognised as a crucial element of the teaching and learning processes and can be described as any information that is provided to a learner about their learning. In short, feedback contributes to learning if pupils are helped to act upon it.

Amanda and Bethany provide children with a range of feedback, some of which can be described as 'surface feedback', and some of which is 'rich feedback'.

For example, both teachers regularly use 'ticks', 'smiley faces' and Bethany also awards 'merits' for what she describes as 'good work'. With regard to non-written feedback, evidence from the study highlights that during a lesson comments such as 'well done!' and more subtle feedback such as body language and smiling at children are also common, for example:

> *The teacher responded highly positively – saying well done! Smiling and nodding head.*
> (Observation 3 of Amanda)

Arguably, such surface feedback does little other than either affirm that work has been marked or is correct, or that information has been exchanged.

However, richer feedback is provided for children by Amanda and Bethany in a number of ways. Firstly, they provide written feedback which indicates whether or not a learning objective has been met. For example, Amanda comments on Susan's piece of work:

> *This is a good attempt at a summary Susan.*

And similarly Bethany comments to Stephen:

> *Stephen, you had a very good understanding of how a non-chronological book works.*
> *Have a Merit. (smiley face)*

In addition both Amanda and Bethany evaluate the work in terms of spelling, grammar and/ or punctuation, even if these were not part of the intended objectives. For example, Bethany comments on a piece of work that was a comprehension activity:

> *Remember proper nouns, like names, need capital letters.*

Amanda and Bethany also use further feedback strategies in order to impact upon teaching and learning.

For example, Bethany explained that she tries to provide pupils with information regarding how they have been successful. She stated that it is important that she frequently makes it explicit to the children that they know what they have not achieved in relation to their own learning, and the learning objectives of the activity and at the same time highlighting what they need to do to be successful. Bethany also said that when giving such feedback, it is also important to highlight the children's successes:

> *I let them know what they have done, what they've achieved, this is important, but they also need to know what they have not achieved and how to get there.*
> *I tend to tell pupils what they have not achieved in relation to their own learning and say what they have achieved and how to get better.*

> *It is useful to describe why an answer is right, it reinforces what they have done. It reinforces, for example, where a comma needs to be.*
>
> (Bethany)

The value of written feedback related specifically to learning objectives was discussed by the children who described how the teacher does this:

> *The teacher writes on your work telling you that you need to improve it to meet the learning objectives.*
>
> (Ryan, Amanda's class)

Amanda and Bethany also provide models to the whole class to provide feedback and this takes place during all parts of the literacy hour. What is of particular interest is that essentially, during taught sessions, it is not the actual model itself that provides the feedback, but the manner in which it is used. For example, the teachers ask children to discuss in pairs either why particular models are effective or to make suggestions for improvements:

> *The teacher then modelled to the class examples of how to use asides in stories. She wrote some examples of her own on the whiteboard and asked the children to talk to each other in pairs about how she had done this.*
>
> (Observation 4 of Bethany)

In addition to providing models to the whole class, the teachers provide models to individual children and they tend to do this through written feedback. Both Amanda and Bethany described how they provide written models for pupils as a means of scaffolding learning and do this in two ways, either while a lesson is in progress or as feedback on completion of an activity. While a lesson is in progress, models with individuals are used similarly to those with the whole class.

For example:

> *Wednesday 15 November, Bethany was working with a group of pupils and Emily was among this group. On Emily's work, titled 'Directed and reported speech,' Emily has written an example of reported speech and Bethany has provided her with a model for direct speech during the lesson: 'I hate him,' she whispered. Emily then continues through the activity providing correct examples of each type of speech.*

However, models that teachers provide pupils with when they are 'distance marking' are different in nature, and serve the purpose of providing exemplars to pupils, and interestingly, although teachers state that they provide models in written marked feedback, evidence of this was very rare. Nevertheless, there were some instances. For example:

> *Simon's independent work dated 16 November. Simon has written: She asked did you find the tunnel. Bethany has modelled this correctly above it: She asked whether she had found the tunnel.*

The pupils also discussed teacher modelling. For example:

If it's just ticks, you don't know what you've done wrong. Like, the connective could be in the wrong place, but you wouldn't know. If she just ticks, you don't know how to make it better. It's much better if she shows you, if she writes it in your book for you and it's there for next time.

(Michelle, Bethany's class)

In addition to using teacher-devised models, the two teachers use examples from the children's work. For example, during whole-class shared work, the following was observed:

The teacher then asked the children to look at the class plan (story plan) ... The teacher then asked the children to discuss with each other a good opening sentence for the middle section of the story. A consensus was made and the rest of the lesson continued in this format, with the teacher scribing, checking and encouraging children to 'check and change'. Throughout this, the teacher continually asked the children to improve each other's work, by considering the choice of verbs and adjectives.

(Observation 6 of Bethany)

However, the use of children's work was noted most frequently when teachers worked with groups, and was particularly evident during plenaries. The teachers used children's models to encourage the rest of the class to assess if lesson objectives had been met. For example, Bethany stated:

I show pupils a range of other pupils' work. When I shared Nigel's story, I read it so that the children couldn't see the spelling errors, well that wasn't part of the criteria and Nigel had done really well. This was to celebrate his work, the rest of the class shared in his success and could see what had made it a good piece of work.

(Bethany)

In addition, Bethany and Amanda were observed using children's work as models in plenaries, for example:

The teacher then used two examples of persuasive writing from Frances and Susan. She read each one in turn. Having finished, she asked the rest of the children to discuss, in pairs, the strengths of each argument, and the differences in style ... The class felt that Frances's was more 'formal' in nature, whereas Susan's was more 'as if she was talking'. The teacher then referred back to the key point of appropriateness and asked the children to consider whether each was appropriate or not. Frances suggested that hers was because it was written for a specific audience. The teacher took Frances's point as a main point for the rest of the class. Exactly, appropriateness means 'fit for purpose'. She explained that you need to think when you are writing, who is it for, who will be reading this? She clarified that there was nothing wrong with Susan's, her arguments are very strong, but her audience would have been different.

(Observation 5 of Amanda)

Data from the study also highlights that the teachers and pupils are engaged in target-setting. They target-set in three key ways. Firstly, the teachers set long-term targets for literacy for the class. These are displayed on classroom walls. Long-term targets are those that the teacher has identified for an extended period of time for the whole class.

Secondly, pupils discussed that teachers set targets for individuals:

The teacher sets me targets after most pieces of work and looks back and tells me if I've done them.

(Ryan, Amanda's class)

Thirdly, there is evidence that pupils engage in setting their own targets. For example, Susan stated that:

I sometimes set myself a target to get better at something, and I'm pleased if I can do it. I don't always tell the teacher, but if I feel that I've done something well, like used some powerful language and that was what I wanted to achieve, then I'll tell her.

(Susan, Amanda's class)

Reflecting on techniques for providing feedback

We have now seen that Amanda and Bethany use a range of techniques to provide feedback to pupils.

When considering feedback and its role in the teaching and learning process, Sadler (1989, p120) states:

Teachers use feedback to make programmatic decisions with respect to readiness, diagnosis and remediation. Students use it to monitor the strengths and weaknesses of their performances, so that aspects associated with success or high quality can be recognised and reinforced, and unsatisfactory aspects modified or improved.

Reflect on your experiences as a learner.

- How important is feedback to you? Why?
- How do you feel when you receive feedback?
- What has been the best feedback that you have received? Why?
- Does feedback that you receive lead to improvement? Why/why not?

Reflect on your experiences as a teacher.

- How important do you think feedback is to the children in your class?

- What strategies do you employ for giving feedback to children? What about your peers?
- Could your practice be enhanced?

Action Point

Collect samples of children's work that you have marked over the past few weeks. Categorise it into 'surface' and 'rich' feedback. What steps could you take to improve your marking's impact on children's learning?

How do Amanda and Bethany consider pupil self-esteem?

The quality and nature of teacher feedback impacts upon pupil self-esteem, and Pollard (1997) suggests that teachers need to 'be positive' with pupils in attempts to build on success, the point being to offer suitable challenges and maximise the use of pupils' achievements. Gipps (1994) suggests that it is not solely feedback from teachers that impacts upon the self-esteem of individuals, but also the feedback from significant others, whereby 'significant others' includes peers and parents. Therefore teachers and pupils need to develop skills in giving feedback to individuals because:

> In the classroom, teachers' verbal and non-verbal behaviour provides information regarding academic content, classroom events, the pupils themselves, etc. It is this information which affects pupil reactions including their perceptions of success and failure.

> (Gipps, 1994, p136)

Amanda and Bethany believe that pupils need to be motivated and have their self-esteem boosted, for example:

> Kids need to know why and be shown how to do things right...also taking the pressure off that person who's not always doing things right by reinforcing the positive. I do really try to do that – give positive rewards. They have to have their self-esteem built up an awful lot, and if they haven't got self-esteem, they're not going to learn...they need confidence, I suppose that is a huge thing, making those people feel valued.

> (Bethany)

They believe that through specifying attainment the pupils know what is expected and are therefore more motivated. For example:

I always try to make it clear to the children what they are doing. I start each lesson with a description of the learning objectives and explain to the children what this means to them. I think this is so important as it lets them know exactly what they have got to do and how they can get there. This motivates them and is good for self-esteem.

(Amanda)

The teachers perceived the notion of motivation and self-esteem as crucial and expressed their desire to provide feedback at all times that would impact positively upon these. For example, Amanda stated:

What I've tried to do with the plenary is to sum the lesson up and check against the criteria to see whether or not they have achieved it, let them think about how they have met the objectives themselves and then as a class. This is a really good way of motivating them.

(Amanda)

Indeed, this notion was endorsed by the children. For example, Simon stated:

I feel chuffed if she says it's 'a merit' or 'excellent' and she's used good comments.

(Simon, Bethany's class)

Julie and Susan also described how particular strategies are motivating:

Originally I was pretty appalled with it [the piece of work], I knew I'd rushed it and mixed things up. The teacher [Amanda] looked at it and told me where it was good, she said 'Julie you've achieved these objectives, well done!' ... I'm pretty pleased with it now!

(Julie, Amanda's class)

If it's a good comment I'm usually happy with it ... She writes comments that are helpful and that are nice.

(Susan, Amanda's class)

Amanda and Bethany also believe that focused written feedback is highly important; however, they described how they struggle to maintain regular focused, written feedback due to time constraints. Furthermore, both teachers believe that specifying improvement in relation to learning objectives is a useful formative strategy but feel concerned that this does not happen with every single piece of work. They are concerned that if children are told too frequently that they need to improve then this will be demotivating and lead to poor self-esteem.

Both teachers described how it is important for pupils to know that their work has been marked by the teacher and as a consequence they employ manageable strategies, such as ticking work, awarding 'merits' and commenting on written work with brief statements, such as 'good' or 'well done!'

Feedback to children is so valuable; if I mark their work or tick it, it's good for self-esteem.

(Amanda)

The class need to know I've marked their work and ticks or merits do this...and motivate them.

(Bethany)

The children in both Amanda's and Bethany's classes made a number of interesting comments in relation to this. They commented on the need for further information, arguing that a brief tick or comment alone provides insufficient information for them and can be perceived as an indicator that the teacher has no time or has rushed her marking. For example, Julie stated:

Teacher ticks are really boring! Good – you know what's right but it's never going to help you – all you're thinking about is the ticks – the teacher's in a hurry, all she's done is one lousy tick that means nothing. Usually if she's in a hurry she'll just rush.

(Julie, Amanda's class)

When the teacher ticks it only tells you it's right. I like getting ticks, but they're not very helpful. Even if it's right, you might not know why.

(Michelle, Bethany's class)

The pupils seem to value positive feedback as a means of boosting self-esteem to a certain extent, but this extrinsic motivator is, in itself, insufficient.

Reflecting on strategies for promoting self-esteem

Current perspectives on teaching and learning (see, for example, Dweck, 2000) allege that the structure of the teaching, through the provision of highly challenging, novel, diverse and authentic tasks, with learning goal orientations, impacts positively on pupil motivation and self-esteem. Dweck (2000, p129), for example, states:

what feeds your esteem – meeting challenges with high effort and using your abilities to help others – is what makes for a productive and constructive life.

We have seen how Amanda and Bethany aim to motivate the children in their classes, and that they place great importance on self-esteem. Let us reflect on their strategies and draw links with our own practice.

• Is it important to consider self-esteem? Why?
• Does your practice consider the needs of all children?
• How can assessment for learning impact upon self-esteem?

Action Point

Often, we do not realise how we behave until we see it for ourselves. It may be useful at this point to consider capturing evidence of your own practice, through perhaps audio-recording or videoing a number of lessons. You may then use the recording to analyse your verbal and non-verbal behaviour.

Stop and Read

Dweck, C.S. (2000) *Self-Theories: Their role in motivation, personality and development.* Philadelphia, PA: Psychology Press.
This book examines how children's (and adults') self-theories illuminate issues of motivation, personality, the self and development. Dweck highlights how students' theories about their intelligence set up the goals that they pursue and how these set up 'adaptive' and 'maladaptive' achievement patterns.

Strategies for developing this content area

In section 1 of this chapter, you have seen how Jane began to turn a rather broad and loosely articulated concern into a more systematic process for improving her practice as a teacher, and better meeting the needs of her students. In section 2, you have seen how Amanda and Bethany use a range of approaches and strategies to support effective assessment practice. You might like to do something similar. The following prompt questions may help you start thinking about this.

* Is there any aspect of your teaching or assessment practice that you would like to improve?
* Have you sometimes found 'off the shelf' solutions not quite what was needed in your particular context?
* Have you ever found that an approach that works really well with one group of students does not work at all with others?
* Do you feel a bit unsure about how to choose appropriate approaches to your teaching?
* Would you like to try to make your pupils more self-evaluative?
* Would you like to work with a group of colleagues to share and develop understanding of effective assessment for learning?
* Do you feel more comfortable teaching literacy than numeracy, for example?
* Is there a particular topic in your subject area that you have always found difficult or boring to teach?
* Is there a particular topic that pupils usually seem to have difficulty with?

Once you have decided on a focus, you might decide to implement and evaluate some strategy in your practice, or you might start from a more exploratory perspective. Chapter 7 will provide further detail of these types of approaches. In either case however, you will need to start building up an evidence base. (In Chapter 7, you will also see a more detailed explanation of the nature of evidence, and the relationship between data and evidence. For the present however, we will use these words relatively interchangeably.)

Start keeping a reflective diary of your teaching sessions. **www.dictionary.com** defines a 'braindump' as *(The act of telling someone) everything one knows about a particular topic.* This is a good way to start off keeping your diary if you are still trying to clarify your focus. Write down all the random thoughts and memories about your teaching sessions and it will soon start to yield some patterns and links which you can begin to make sense of.

Make sure your diary is not merely descriptive; otherwise, you will get little in the way of insight from it. Jenny Moon (2002) provides an excellent framework for developing deep and critical reflection on your practice, and follows this up with an example (Resources 9 and 10). Likewise, Mason (2002, pp42–3) provides some excellent illustrations of how you can ask questions of your practice during a reconnaissance phase.

If you are implementing and evaluating a particular strategy, your diary entries will probably be more focused, but will still require some work in order to collate and analyse the evidence. At the end of one or two weeks (the time period depends on how much contact you have with the group, or how often you teach the subject/topic), try to extract the key points emerging from the accounts. Are there patterns? Links? Common triggers for certain types of events? Particular approaches which seem to stimulate your pupils more than others?

The big question now is – How can you make sense of this? What can you do about it? Are you sure you have the whole picture (or at least a balanced one)? How might you supplement it? List other ways in which you could gather data about your classroom practice. Now continue your diary-keeping for a further few weeks and focusing on what has been emerging as the key points, but in addition, start also adding other sources and perspectives.

You might now have the following types of data.

- Your own reflective diary.
- Peer/critical friend observations of your teaching.
- Notes from planning sessions/meetings about your teaching.
- Evidence from the pupils you teach (which could be in the form of samples of their work, comments they have made, diaries that they have kept, etc.
- Notes from focus group meetings with pupils.

You can add to this list as appropriate.

After a further period of time (perhaps another two weeks or so) you can start to think of what you have gathered as an evidence base, and use this as the basis for drawing up an evidence-informed action plan that is personal and personalised to your needs and the needs of your pupils.

You will have seen that Jane's project was a simple, but compelling illustration of the potency of undertaking action research. Having started from an initial premise that reflecting on her own teaching, and augmenting that reflection by other perceptions and sources of evidence would place her in a position to devise strategies through which she could attempt to improve her practice, the project soon began to run with a life of its own. The ongoing refocusing of an action research approach became the preserve of the class group, not just Jane. This is an important step in strengthening your evidence base as your project continues.

If, like many postgraduate students, getting a starting focus is proving challenging for you, you might want to use your diary more broadly at first, and see what begins to emerge as something that is both professionally interesting to you, and significant in your practice. Remember that:

> *Action research is open ended. It does not begin with a fixed hypothesis. It begins with an idea that you develop. The research process is the developmental process of following through the idea, seeing how it goes, and continually checking whether it is in line with what you wish to happen. Seen in this way, action research is a form of self evaluation. It is used widely in professional contexts such as appraisal, mentoring and self assessment.*

(www.jeanmcniff.com/booklet1.html#2)

It is not only usual, it is, in fact appropriate that you start with more of an idea, than a clear question. What is imperative though, is the focus on your own practice in your own context, and the ability to make a difference through doing this. An excellent example (quoted below) of how this idea can be reformulated as an action research question is given by Riel (2007).

> *Consider this question:*
> If I listen to students, will I have better understanding of them?
>
> *This question suggests an action and possible outcome but is vague both in the description of the action and in the possible outcome.*
>
> *Now consider:*
> If I set up community circle time to listen to students describe their learning experiences in my classroom, in what ways, if any, will the information about their learning processes help me redesign the way I teach?
>
> *Now it is clear what the researcher intends to do and what a possible outcome might be. In listening to students, the researcher might discover information that will lead directly to an experiment in instructional design or might refocus the overall goal to one that was not apparent when the researcher started the quest.*

(Riel, 2007)

An excellent scaffold/framework to assist you in turning your reflections and concerns into a project that can be used for your assignment can be found at: **www.sitesupport.org/ actionresearch/ses3_act2_pag1.shtml**

You can see from both McNiff's description, and Riel's example, that action research projects provide a simple, but powerful way through which teachers can address the personalised agenda.

Table 3.1 demonstrates how Jane moved her analyses of and decisions about practice into actions for changed practice.

Table 3.1 Jane's analysis of decisions and actions

The decision	The action
Jane decided that she could address her students' learning needs more effectively if she listened to their reflections on their learning and her teaching	1. Jane planned to make it easy for her students to give her this feedback, and built in a simple system for doing this. She gave time at the end of each teaching session for it, and encouraged her students to write down their feedback, either in a reflective diary, or on sticky notes, that the students themselves could collate into a 'feedback wall' 2. Jane planned sessions where she would respond to her students' reflections, so that they realised that she felt these reflections to be important
Jane decided that she was depending too much on one specific approach to her teaching (and that there was an overload of PowerPoint), and that this did not meet the needs of her learners	1. Jane began to build in alternative, more discourse-based teaching strategies which allowed for more discussion in the hopes that this would lead to deeper understanding 2. Jane decided that while she would still continue to plan her teaching sessions carefully, she would try to become attuned to feedback from her students during lessons, so that small, but vital adjustments could be made if necessary

It was important at this stage for Jane to consider some systematic way of monitoring and evaluating the changes that were taking place in her practice. She decided to try out her new strategies for a one-month period, carefully monitoring the impact that they might have. She continued to keep her reflective diary, as did her students. She planned also to interview her students towards the end of the month to discuss issues in greater depth with them. Because she has also noticed an unexpected impact on student performance, she also planned to keep samples of their homework and any class test results. Together, this body of evidence would, through its collation and analysis, supported by reading the appropriate academic literature, help her assess the effect of the changes she had been making.

The study of Amanda and Bethany was completed by an outside researcher, and while it gives less insight into their deliberative and reflective processes, you can see how the researcher has encouraged them to describe and explain their practice, and has compared and contrasted this with the experiences of children in their class. This study has a very clear focus – assessment for learning – and its primary purpose is to show how a better understanding and practice of assessment for learning can have a positive impact on classroom practice and children's learning. (Jane's study was a search to find a way of improving her teaching, and she had no strategy to implement at the start.)

Once again, you can see the systematic approach to gathering evidence about professional practice, and the use of theory in exploring and explaining it. Through an approach like this, you not only get a better picture of what professional practice is like (which is particularly important as an early-career teacher), but you also begin to understand why it is like that, and what theoretical underpinnings support it.

Assignments

Suggested assignments to address this content area

When you undertake your MTL, you will be encouraged to engage in school-based practice development work, which can be the basis for assignments/assessment opportunities for MTL modules. The strategies above may get you thinking about how you might focus, and how you might gather evidence to use as part of your assessed work.

You might find the following list of action research studies I have supervised helpful in raising your awareness of the types of study you might choose to engage in and helping you to arrive at a specific focus. In all cases, the study produces a personalised response to issues of teaching and learning (or in some cases, to the management of educational issues). You will notice also, that these questions have been asked by teachers at various stages in their careers; indeed, some are in senior leadership roles. All, however, have found that this approach is one which allows them to respond specifically to the needs of their own situations and contexts. By asking a question about yourself in your own professional context, by using responses to that question to make appropriate changes in your practice, you have the potential for making teaching and learning a highly personalised experience, and to also produce evidence of the impact your own professional development is making on your practice and pupil achievement.

- Using action research to improve my teaching of numeracy.
- Exploring the issues in managing a pastoral team, in order to improve my own leadership.
- How can I promote self-determination in young people with learning difficulties?
- How can I promote effective learning and teaching in my Year 11 examination class?
- How can I promote better parent–teacher relationships in the context of a special school?
- Addressing underachievement in my class: giving my students a voice.
- How can I bridge the gap between effective teaching and effective learning in my class?
- How can I promote pupil curiosity and inquiry in my science teaching?

When you embark upon your MTL, an aspect of your development will be to develop your understanding of theoretical perspectives of teaching and learning, and you will be encouraged to demonstrate this through reflecting on your own practice, which may form the basis for assignments and/or assessment opportunities. The following list may provide you with some useful starting points for reflecting on theory and practice associated with assessment for learning.

* How do I develop self-evaluation in my daily lessons?
* How can I provide rich written feedback to pupils?
* Developing my understanding of pupils' perceptions of peer evaluation.
* What are my colleagues doing? Sharing and developing effective practice.
* Using case study research to improve my ability to provide timely feedback to pupils.
* How does my written feedback affect children's motivation?
* Formative use of summative tests.

Summary

At the end of this chapter you should have:
* **improved your understanding of teaching and learning theories;**
* **understood ways in which personalised learning can become part of your professional practice;**
* **understood how personalised learning is linked to the core standards for teachers;**
* **identified the means by which you could undertake some small-scale action research in order to improve your teaching to better meet the learning needs of your students;**
* **developed your understanding of assessment through having questioned some assumptions and reflected on your own practice;**
* **developed your understanding of assessment for learning;**
* **understood that assessment for learning is embedded in practice;**
* **identified strengths and areas for development with regard to your own practice;**
* **understood that a case study approach can open doors of enquiry into practice.**

Further reading

Moyles, J. (2007) Beginning Teaching: Beginning learning. Maidenhead: Open University Press/ McGraw-Hill.

Schön, D. (1983) *The Reflective Practitioner: How professionals think in action*. New York: Basic Books.

Somekh, B. (2006) *Action Research: A methodology for change and development*. Maidenhead: Open University Press/McGraw-Hill.

Winter, R. (1989) *Learning From Experience: Principles and practice In action-research*. Abingdon: Falmer.

Useful websites

Qualifications and Curriculum Development Agency **www.qcda.gov.uk**
The Standards Site /**www.standards.dfes.gov.uk**

CHAPTER 4

Content area 2: Subject knowledge, curriculum and curriculum development

Teachers also continue to express a need for more training in using information and communications technology (ICT) in their teaching, and for strengthening and/or updating their skills and knowledge in curriculum subject areas.

(GTC, 2007)

Chapter Objectives

By the end of this chapter, you should have:
- been supported in devising strategies for developing your subject knowledge;
- had opportunities to work with others in order to improve your pedagogy;
- explored a range of pedagogical approaches, including ICT-supported teaching and learning;
- become familiar with developments in your own area of specialism;
- become aware of a range of policy and curriculum initiatives in education.

Links to the professional core standards

As a teacher, you need to make sure that you are always up to date in knowledge of your own subject or phase specialism, and also of curriculum and policy requirements. This section of your MTL will address the following core standards. Appendix 1 will show you a table illustrating how you can progress from core to the higher standards through addressing this content area.

Professional attributes
C3

Professional knowledge and understanding
C15, C16 and C17

Professional Skills
C27

This chapter is in two sections, and addresses content area 2. Section 1 will focus on subject knowledge for teaching, presenting a number of short case studies illustrating ways in which teachers can update and improve their subject knowledge as part of their ongoing professional development. Section 2 will look at a range of curriculum issues, again through the use of case studies. It will also introduce you to the external environment relating to subject and curriculum knowledge, policy and statutory requirements

Section 1: Subject knowledge for teaching

Introduction

This content area is wide-ranging in breadth and scope, and obviously some of it will be more relevant to you, depending on your phase, subject and context, and indeed depending on your current concerns. You will notice that this content area also contains references to issues of teaching and learning, assessment and SEN. We will not focus specifically on these issues in this chapter, as all are covered in more detail in the other chapters of this book.

During your teaching career, subject knowledge is something you will continuously have to update. For most teachers, membership of subject associations, attendance at INSET courses, the reading of professional journals and publications, and consultation with colleagues all form a key way in which you can do this. Some of the case studies in the next section illustrate ways in which teachers have managed to do this. It is worthwhile at this stage to also point out a little more about the benefits offered by subject associations. You can find an overview of the full range of national subject associations in the Council for Subject Associations (CfSA) web page.

If you read through the introductory pages on this site, you will begin to see the strategic importance of subject associations, and their role in supporting excellence in both subject knowledge and pedagogy. As an overview body, CfSA also has strategic input in policy-making, and as such can inform curriculum development and change. From the CfSA page, you can find links to your relevant subject association where you are likely to find a number of key benefits of membership listed. Let us take one such association, the Association for Science Education (ASE), the largest subject association, as an illustrative example of the benefits of membership. You will initially see a range of membership benefits including journals and other research publications, CPD opportunities, conference attendance, and the support of a national network of colleagues. Other associations offer similar benefits, and many offer regional events on a regular basis. It is worth considering membership of the relevant association, and indeed discussing this with your colleagues at school.

As a practising teacher, you also need to familiarise yourself with the range of statutory requirements for your subject or phase area, and support available to you in this respect. While your more senior colleagues at school may well provide you with examination syllabi and other frameworks, it is important that you are proactive in keeping abreast of changes in the statutory framework. The web page of the Qualifications and Curriculum Development Agency (QCDA) allows you to navigate the site in a way that is appropriate to your own contextualised needs, be it as an NQT, a subject leader, a specialist infant teacher or whatever. On this site you will find details of examination frameworks, guidance materials for schools, examples of schemes of work, support in devising, developing and customising schemes of work

The following case studies show a range of ways in which some early-career teachers updated their subject knowledge in a way that enhanced their teaching.

Case Study

The NQT cluster

Lorna, Claire, Gill, Martin and Jack are all newly qualified teachers of history in the same local authority but at different schools. Both the authority and the schools are forward looking in that they have arranged for the five NQTs to meet together on regular occasions to discuss both subject knowledge and the pedagogy within their subject area. Richert (1991) suggests that novice teachers must be given numerous and a variety of chances to meet and listen to one another think aloud but due to the frenetic nature of teaching and the added pressure of the induction year this rarely happens.

These NQTs are fortunate that this opportunity has been afforded them and they are determined to explore how they can progress through collaboration. At their first meeting they decide to consider their individual needs through a concept-mapping exercise. The concept map is a product of 25 years of research and development, focusing on helping students to learn how to learn. The idea of the concept map as a data-collection tool originated with the work of Joseph Novak and colleagues at Cornell University. The points that the NQTs considered were:

- their perceived strengths;
- their perceived areas for development and concerns as to how these will be addressed;
- how to develop their subject knowledge;
- the development of professional relationships with colleagues and pupils.

At the first meeting the NQTs identified their strengths as follows.

- Lorna initially identified her strengths in terms of her subject knowledge, organisation, positive outlook and communication skills.
- Claire considered at the outset of her teaching career that her strengths were identified in terms of her organisational skills, high standards and expectations, her ability to be a team player, communication skills and her planning.
- Gill identified her strengths in planning, working in a team and her subject knowledge.
- Martin viewed his strengths as being approachable, a good communicator and the ability to form good relationships with both staff and pupils.
- Jack identified his strengths in his enthusiasm, humour and organisation.

In terms of identified professional development needs the following were evident.

- Lorna identified behaviour management as an area of concern. She also identified the necessity to produce 'a good quality supply of resources' and the requirement to meet the national standards for NQTs.
- Claire's initial concerns were not being a form tutor and the lack of GCSE classes in her timetable.
- At the outset of the year Gill had concerns about behaviour management, being a form tutor, school routines and expectations and time management.
- Martin recognised his professional development needs as the ability to set personal targets and to enhance his promotion prospects to the head of department. Martin's reflections centred on how he was 'still trying to be the best history teacher I can possibly be' and his only concern was to meet the needs of his current classes.
- Areas for professional development were identified by Jack in the fields of increased subject knowledge and awareness of syllabi.

Reflecting on areas for development

In the case study above Lorna, Claire, Gill, Martin and Jack were able to recognise different strengths and areas for development. Lorna's subject knowledge was an important feature of her strength and only identified by one other member of the group (Gill). Claire had planning high on her list of strengths while Martin was a good communicator. Jack clearly brings with him his humour: a necessity in the induction year. Through identifying their own strengths and areas for development, and through the subsequent series of focused meetings they were able to share expertise and contribute to each other's and their own practice development. Their own comments on their processes illustrate the extent to which this was important as the induction year progressed.

Lorna:
Sharing ideas about how to approach problems has been helpful. It is great to hear about ideas that have worked and that you can adopt.

Claire:
We encouraged each other to reflect upon lessons during all meetings but the two sessions on good/ bad lessons that we had taught and creativity are most memorable.

Gill:
By becoming reflective practitioners we were constantly reflecting on [our own] practice and that of others at the meetings.

Martin:

It was really good when Gill and Lorna led the meeting on subject knowledge and the sharing of resources and lesson plans has helped all of us.

Jack:

Sharing ideas about how to approach problems in general as well as subject specific has been helpful. I feel more confident now in my subject knowledge.

What is of particular significance in this case study is the way in which, collectively, these NQTs have undertaken a needs assessment in their new context, and have now identified what they need to do in order to improve various aspects of their practice. You might like to discuss with your colleagues how this starting point could be further developed to meet your needs as you work through your MTL.

Action Point

Study the strengths and areas of development of the group and consider how they can be mutually supportive. How can they share good practice and contribute to the needs of others in the group? Consider also how this group should develop in order to sustain momentum in the sharing of ideas.

In particular, however, consider how, as a group they could share and develop subject knowledge and pedagogy. Might some of their other concerns (for example, resources, meeting NQT standards, behaviour management and 'being the best history teacher') be rooted in issues of subject knowledge and pedagogy? Discuss with peers and mentors and coaches how improving subject knowledge and pedagogy might impact upon these aspects of practice. How would they know whether it was having an impact? Discuss how they would plan to critically reflect on and review their own developing practice.

You may be able to use this type of structure while you work with fellow participants on MTL.

Stop and Read

Phillips, I. (2008) *Teaching History: Developing as a reflective teacher*. London: Sage.

This book is aimed at those training to be history teachers through the PGCE and Graduate Teacher Programme (GTP) but as the induction year may be viewed as a continuum of training it will prove useful to those in their early careers. It was reviewed as follows:

If you are an NQT or a new head of department, consider asking your school to buy you a copy as part of your induction. If you have been teaching for a while and need something that will generate discussion at school this book will help and some of Ian's comments will make you laugh; that wry laugh when you recognise a familiar situation and realise you have been offered an insightful analysis of it.

Case Study

Learning from experience

This case study illustrates a more formalised approach into practice enquiry following a needs identification. Here, both Maria and her more experienced head of department, Harry, both identify personalised learning needs, and undertake enquiry into changing practice.

Before you read this case study, think of your teacher training, your school placements, and your current role in school. You will have had opportunities to observe some more experienced colleagues, and no doubt will have found this a valuable learning experience. Think of the teachers you admire and have admired, and try to articulate what qualities they had, which makes you consider them 'good teachers'. I asked a number of recently qualified teachers to list the features that they thought important, and among their responses were the following.

- Knows their subject.
- Makes lessons interesting.
- Uses a range of teaching strategies including ICT.
- Enthusiastic and loves what they do.
- Encourages all the pupils in the class.
- Has a good relationship with pupils.
- Good class control.

What would you add to this list?

Reis, writing in 2009, lists ten qualities which he claims, from informal research and discussions with teachers, provide not a definitive list, but a set of points around which to think about good teaching. Top of his list is *good teachers really want to be good teachers*. I think this is an important one for us to focus on, or indeed in as I would prefer, *good teachers really want to be better teachers*. It is tempting to think that this is something you need to do as you are still learning your art as a teacher, but the reality is that this is something good teachers do throughout their teaching careers. Let me now introduce you to Harry and Maria.

Harry has been teaching English for many years, and is known in his school as an excellent teacher. He knows his subject well, has good class control, and students achieve good results in his class. He is head of his subject area, and leads a team of teachers that has seen little change in recent years. The department is considered to be strong and stable. Ofsted reports are consistently good. Harry, however, feels that they are perhaps too stable, and have settled into a little bit of a rut. Despite consistently good reports, he feels that he would like to encourage more boys in the department to take English literature for GCSE and A level. He has not, however, done anything about this.

Maria joins the department as a newly qualified teacher and feels somewhat intimidated by the experience of the other department members, and her own lack of experience. She is however, very enthusiastic about her subject, and very eager to learn more about teaching it from these people she considers to be experts. Her first six weeks in post are extremely busy. She has new people to get to know, and new year groups to teach. All in all, she feels she is on a very steep learning curve. After her first half-term holiday, Harry asks to meet her to discuss how she has settled into the new job and school. The following points are raised in the course of the meeting.

- Maria sometimes feels that she 'goes about teaching things in the wrong way'. In particular, she feels uncomfortable teaching poetry, and feels that she doesn't know enough outside set reading lists.
- Harry has overheard comments from Year 9 boys (and also girls) that English literature is 'dead good' with 'that new teacher'. He wonders if this might affect the uptake of English literature at GCSE, and also wonders what makes her classes so good.
- Maria would like to plan more outings to theatre and cinema with her classes, but isn't sure how acceptable this would be in this rather conservative department. In fact, she is somewhat afraid that it might be seen as frivolous.

Reflecting on experience

In the case study above Harry and Maria acknowledge the different strengths they both bring to teaching. As a relatively newly qualified teacher, Maria was able to draw on Harry's extensive experience, and ask his advice on strategies for making the teaching of poetry better in her lessons. In addition, he was able to recommend ways in which she could supplement her own knowledge of poetry, which made her feel more confident in her teaching. He was also able to recommend, again from his experience, ways of introducing poetry, and suggest suitable poems to start with for lower-ability pupils. In discussion with Maria however, he realises that she has some very interesting approaches to teaching drama, and begins to reflect on his own teaching. He particularly thinks of his approach to teaching poetry, which he feels is competent, very well informed, but perhaps could be livelier. Perhaps it could benefit from a fresher, more innovative, more interactive approach. Perhaps Maria might suggest some strategies he could use.

They devise an action plan for the second half-term, which includes regular collaborative planning and evaluation of lessons. In addition however, they agree to co-teach a set of lessons, which they will use as the basis for reflection. He also arranges for her to work in this way with other department members. Maria hopes to use these reflections as evidence to show how she is meeting some of the professional standards.

Overall, Maria's English teaching was greatly enhanced by working closely with her mentor, and other experienced staff. The collaborative planning, monitoring and evaluating of her lessons provided her with a rich evidence base about the impact of these changes on her pupils. The corollary of this was that teaching in the department experienced a rejuvenation, and began to review teaching and learning experiences, explore more innovative approaches, and planned a drama club and workshop. This provided a very clear indication to her, and to Harry, that the changes have impacted positively on the outcomes for pupils in the department.

Action Point

What do you think Harry and Maria might have learned from this meeting? Working with your mentor, discuss the learning points, and develop an action plan for the second half-term. Take into account the points both Harry and Maria have raised, and suggest strategies that might benefit them both, and also the department and pupils.

Stop and Read

Child, A. and Merrill, S. (2005) *Developing as a Secondary School Mentor*. Exeter: Learning Matters.

Although this text is written primarily for mentors, this book gives an insight into the mentoring relationship, and the case studies presented provide a simple illustration of many of the ways in which the mentoring relationship can provide a rich source of support in your early professional development.

Evans, C., Midgley, A., Rigby, P., Warham, L. and Woolnough, P. (2009) *Teaching English*. London: Sage.

This book deals with a range of strategies for the effective teaching of English to pupils across the age and ability ranges. It gives guidance on the planning of effective lessons and other learning experiences, and offers support for managing and assessing learning.

Case Study

Laura branches out

Laura was a newly qualified teacher with her first class of Year 5 children. She had a specialism in PE but felt a little overwhelmed when it came to teaching the other foundation subjects and religious education (FSRE). During her one-year PGCE degree at university she had 176 face-to-face hours of core subjects but only 88 of FSRE and so felt that although the tutors provided stimulating sessions with excellent lesson ideas, the subject matter of each area was limited. This was a particular worry when it came to teaching religious Education (RE) as she was very worried about what the local authority syllabus required of her and her lack of subject knowledge in some of the specific aspects of it. She recalled that during her PGCE, one of her independent study tasks had been to improve her subject knowledge through directed reading of texts such as *The Handbook of Living Traditions* (2004). However, now in her first job, she was conscious of how much she still had to learn and was also afraid of inadvertently offending children and parents through ill-informed teaching.

Many teachers feel worried about teaching RE and feel that they lack detailed subject knowledge about the many different religions and faiths. In this respect, Laura's worries were similar to those of many other experienced teachers (McCreery *et al.*, 2008). After talking with other members of staff Laura realised that she wasn't alone in her insecurities but as the local authority didn't have an RE adviser, she did not have a specialist to turn to for advice. She realised that she needed to try to find a more proactive way to develop her own professional knowledge.

The first thing Laura chose to do was an audit of her knowledge of the six different faith traditions. She was familiar with doing audits for the core subjects while at university and chose to adapt an audit model that she has used during one of the RE sessions from her PGCE.

She looked through the RE resource box in the school and took out the religious and secular artefacts. She sorted them into the different faith traditions and then made notes on what she thought they were.

To help her focus on what she needed to research, she used three questions.

1. What does the artefact show me? – She wrote down exactly what she saw, i.e. a picture of a boy with an elephant's head with four arms.
2. What doesn't the artefact show me? – Who the boy is and why he looks the way he does. Is he a god?
3. What do I need to find out? – gods in Hinduism, religious icons.

In doing this, Laura began to 'paint a picture' of her own subject knowledge. She realised what areas she was strong in, and where there were gaps. She used this to guide her in some independent subject knowledge enhancement research, using texts and websites as appropriate. While doing this she also remembered having heard about the National Association of Teachers of Religious Education (NATRE), and made enquiries about what they could offer. She approached her head teacher to explore the possibility of the school supporting her membership fee. On joining, she found she had access to a range of courses, research publications, a broad professional network and access to local support too. She began to attend some local events, and through meeting other local members, began to work in a collaborative cluster with two other teachers who shared her concerns. Together they accessed, through NATRE, a body of research reports on the teaching of different faiths, and on the basis of this, developed a unit of work using a broad range of subject materials, and a variety of pedagogical approaches. Additionally, they decided to evaluate the implementation of the unit in each of three schools, and agreed to share the outcomes of this with each other, the rest of the local group, and their own school colleagues, and raise critical questions around the reports. Their final meeting agenda had one item: 'What, if anything, could we have done differently or better?'

Reflecting on subject knowledge

In the case study above Laura was brave in admitting that although she is now qualified she still isn't able to know everything about how to teach aspects of a core subject. The fact that she was able to discover that other members of staff had similar worries made her realise that a teacher is always learning throughout his/her career. She used what she knew was a strength of hers, her organisation and ability to undertake research independently, to address what she knew was a weakness, and to act on her own initiative.

Having completed the audit, and started working with the local cluster group, she and her colleagues in school realised that in addition to now having improved her subject knowledge and pedagogy, she had also become more confident as both a teacher and a learner. She was subsequently asked to present a twilight staff development session about the use of self-audit as a mechanism for planning development, and was able to introduce to her school a wide range of both subject and pedagogy resources for RE teaching. A further interesting outcome of this was the impact it had on Laura's career pathway. The deputy head of the school was the RE co-ordinator, and asked Laura to also work closely with her in a shadowing/advisory capacity, given her developing subject expertise in RE. Within a few years she was appointed co-ordinator for PE in recognition of her leadership skills.

Action Point

Reflect on some of the sessions in university and consider how they can help you now. Are there any tips that you picked up on how to develop your own subject knowledge? Make a portfolio of resources and lesson ideas that you can refer to when planning. How might you now extend this systematically to draw on broader knowledge and practice base in order to enhance your own understanding?

How might you plan to evaluate the impact of such an initiative on your teaching and the outcomes for your pupils? What types of evidence might you need, and how might you collect that evidence? Are there any difficulties in making claims for improvements in your practice?

Stop and Read

McCreery E., Palmer S. and Voiels, V. (2008) *Teaching Religious Education: Primary and early years*. Exeter: Learning Matters.
This text is useful as a starting point for RE and provides good advice on the subject itself and also on how to teach it. It also has a small information section that can help with general basic information about the faith traditions.

Webster, M. (2009) *Creative Approaches to Teaching Primary Religious Education*. London: Pearson Education.
This text, which is aimed at trainee teachers and NQTs, explores religious education as a cross-curricular subject, providing an extensive list of resources that will support creative approaches to your teaching of RE. There is also a chapter on developing subject knowledge.

Section 2: Curriculum and curriculum development

This section will focus on curriculum and curriculum development, again through the use of case studies. Whether you work in primary or secondary education, you will be aware of major and ongoing changes to the curriculum, and part of your professional role is to keep abreast of these changes, and plan your professional development in a way that enables you to work effectively within new frameworks.

Introduction

Curriculum and curriculum development
The indicative content list for the MTL indicates just how diverse this section is, itemising a number of points within its scope, including:

- what is planned to be taught to enable all children/young people to maximise their learning;

- sum total of formal and informal areas of learning;
- knowledge, understanding, skills;
- curriculum design;
- National Curriculum developments;
- 14–19 reform and the suite of new qualifications;
- planning progression of, and personalising learning opportunities for, all children/young people, including children with SEN and disability and G&T learners;
- learning in contexts beyond the classroom.

The design and development of curricula is something that you may, as a newly qualified teacher, feel somewhat remote from. Perhaps you consider the curriculum to be the prescribed syllabus or specification for the subject or key stage that you teach. It is also the case however, that a more complete understanding of the word 'curriculum' is the sum of all the planned experiences that inform learning and development. If this is taken as our definition, then it becomes increasingly obvious that the curriculum is something that we have a more interactive relationship with than may be thought. As teachers, we are not simply passive recipients of it. We mediate and manage it through our daily practice as teachers. We bring to it our own values, attitudes and beliefs, and recognise also the values, beliefs and attitudes of our colleagues and our pupils.

However, as professionals, we also need to keep abreast of changes in the curriculum structure. In some cases, as suggested above, there may be an updating of subject content, and as teachers, we need to continuously update our knowledge in this respect. However, it is also the case that national initiatives bring change which is broader in scope, and may significantly reshape the structure of educational provision. We shall now look at some such initiatives; the 14–19 Framework in the secondary sector, the Primary Framework for Literacy and Mathematics, and ICT which is across all subjects and phases.

14–19 developments

The 2005 White Paper *14–19 Education and Skills* heralded the introduction of wide-ranging reforms. The reforms started in 2006 with new GCSEs in science subjects, and are planned to continue until 2013. It is likely that these reforms will impact on most, if not all, secondary teachers.

A significant change in provision is the choices available to pupils over the age of 14. At ages 14 and 16, pupils will be able to choose one of three routes: the diploma, GCSE/A-level respectively or an apprenticeship. At 16, there is also the option to be in work with dedicated time for training. By the age of 18, it is envisaged that young people will either be qualified for further education or training, or be ready to go into skilled work

The diploma

The new diploma qualifications are still in the early stages, and developments will continue over the next few years, with a predicted 17 subjects available by September 2011. These diplomas are described by the direct.gov diploma website as ... *a new qualification for 14–*

19 year olds, the Diploma is a combination of existing qualifications and purpose-designed qualifications to make up a two year course. The Diploma is designed to support your next move – whether that's further study at school or college, work-related training, going on to university or a job with training.

These diplomas are designed to prioritise the core skills of English, mathematics and ICT, while developing life and social skills such as teamwork. For students taking these diplomas, education will occur in their own classrooms, in other educational locations like partner schools or colleges, and in work-based settings.

The diplomas can be studied at the three levels:

* foundation;
* higher;
* advanced.

There is also a progression diploma, equivalent to 2.5 A levels, and plans for an extended diploma from 2011. The extended diploma builds on the diploma while offering extra mathematics and English, and additional specialist learning.

The diplomas and extended diplomas have equivalency as shown in Table 4.1.

Table 4.1 Equivalency of diplomas and extended diplomas

Level	Diploma	Extended Diploma
Foundation	5 GCSE grades D to G	7 GCSE grades D to G
Higher	7 GCSE grades A* to C	9 GCSE grades A* to C
Advanced	3.5 A levels	4.5 A levels

Apprenticeships

An Apprenticeship is a structured programme of training which gives young people the opportunity to work for an employer, learn on the job and build up knowledge and transferable skills that will be needed throughout a working life.
(www.teachernet.gov.uk/teachingandlearning/14to19/Apprenticeships/)

The apprenticeship option is accessed in one of three ways.

* Direct application to employers.
* Learning and Skills Council Apprenticeships Helpline.
* Connexions.

Since May 2004, provision has been made for a range of entry points.

- Young Apprenticeships for 14– to 16-year-olds.
- Pre-Apprenticeships – based on the popular Entry to Employment programme (at level 1).
- Apprenticeships (at level 2).
- Advanced Apprenticeships (at level 3).
- Opening up of Adult Apprenticeships by lifting the age limit of 25.

The provision of the young apprenticeship entry point is to suit the needs of those 14–16–year-olds who wish to pursue industry-specific vocational programmes outside of school. The structure of the apprenticeship route provides progression, and an opportunity to progress to further studies or foundation degrees where appropriate. You can get up-to-date information about apprenticeships at **www.apprenticeships.org.uk/**

Flexibility of provision
DCSF, QCDA and the Learning and Skills Council (LSC) have been working closely to map commonality among the diploma, additional and specialist learning, and relevant apprenticeship frameworks. Work continues on this to provide clear guidelines for progression, so that pupils on one route know how they may progress to another. Once again, sites such as QCDA, DCSF and Teachernet provide recent and relevant information.

What else is happening?
The development of diplomas is part of a more general review of education for 11–19-year-olds, and further developments are planned as follows.

- A general review of the post-14 curriculum.
- Strengthening existing qualifications (GCSE reform; GCE reform; development of extended project).
- Modernising the exams system.

As before, sites such as QCDA, DCSF and Teachernet provide the most up-to-date information, and support and guidance materials.

Other developments

The Primary Framework for literacy and mathematics
> *It is imperative that all our children develop these basic skills [literacy and mathematics] to sustain their learning and the confidence to access the curriculum as they move into secondary education.*
>
> (Lord Adonis, Introduction to Primary Framework, 2006)

In 1998, a national framework, designed to improve standards of literacy and numeracy in primary schools, was launched. Launched in schools in 1999, the National Literacy and the

National Numeracy strategies were intended to improve the literacy and numeracy achievements of children of primary school age. The renewed Primary Framework (renaming numeracy as mathematics), implemented in 2006, recognised the progress that had been made in the preceding years, but also saw the need to address what was seen as a lack of sustained progress across the board. In addition, it recognised the prime significance of Key Stage 1 experiences as *the major milestone on the way to children being confident in literacy and mathematics by the time they leave their primary schools* (Lord Adonis, Introduction to Primary Framework, 2006).

As a primary school teacher, you will already be familiar with this, and should now be building on and consolidating your experiences in order to improve your teaching of both literacy and numeracy. The Framework document provides you with planning and assessing resources, and together with the relevant co-ordinators in your school you should now be taking a more proactive approach to your planning, teaching and assessing of these core curricular areas. You should notice first of all, that the outcomes allow for a clear understanding of pupil progression, personalisation of approach, the use of early intervention if indicated, and other measures, all designed to enhance achievement. In order to help you access a range of support for your own teaching and learning in this respect, the Framework is available electronically, providing links to a range of planning, teaching and assessment resources. Specific guidance and support are provided in areas where children are often found to have difficulty, although the degree to which this is used is left to the professional judgement of the teacher. Target setting plays a key part in this process and you should now be actively involved in setting realistic, yet challenging targets for your pupils.

Stop and Read

You can find a range of useful material in relation to the Primary Framework at
www.standards.dfes.gov.uk/primaryframeworks/
A range of resources and supporting frameworks to assist your own planning is available at
www.nationalstrategies.standards.dcsf.gov.uk/primary/primaryframework

ICT

We must support innovation in the market by improving our knowledge of where elearning works particularly well, and update our standards for pedagogic quality, accessibility and safety. And we must keep the curriculum moving, to take advantage of new methods in all subject areas, and to keep demanding a better response from the technology.

(Harnessing Technology: Transforming learning and children's services, DfES, 2005)

Updating our standards for pedagogic quality sets a challenge to us as teachers to use ICT appropriately in our teaching, and in a way that demonstrably enhances the learning opportunities for children.

In many lessons I have observed, the ICT component was very much an 'add-on', and in truth, seemed to have little pedagogical justification or coherence with the general pedagogy of the lesson. Additionally, it often brought no extra interest factor, or motivational factor to lessons. Students have seen it all before. Some students comment on the 'sameness' of interactive whiteboard use from class to class. In many ways, their comments were the equivalent of the 'death by PowerPoint' comments at many INSET events and presentations. Before you embark on planning lessons with ICT involvement, you should read some recent studies on the use and impact of ICT. Chapter 10 of Somekh's book (2007) *Pedagogy and Learning with ICT*, reports on the ImpaCT2 project, which ran from 1999 to 2002. The aims of the project were as follows.

1. To identify the impacts of networked technologies on the school and out-of-school environment.
2. To determine whether or not this impact affects the educational attainment of students aged 8–16 in English schools.
3. To provide information that would assist in the formation of national, local and school policies on the deployment of ICT.

As part of their research they collected and analysed 4000 concept maps from school children aged between 9 and 16. A significant finding of the study was the degree to which ICT provides a range of learning tools very different to those previously available to support student learning. Somekh cites the work of Vygotsky (1978) and Wertsch (1998) in support of the theory that such *radical changes in tools mediate human activity and radically change working methods and outcomes*. As such, she claims, *megachange in schools is more or less inevitable as a result* (Somekh 2007, p176).

It is interesting to review this research (and indeed read the rest of this highly informative and thought-provoking book) in the light of the current designation of those born after 1980 as 'digital natives', and those born before that time designated 'digital immigrants'. This classification supposes that there is homogeneity in those born post-1980 in terms not just of their ICT capabilities, but more importantly in their 'fluency' in their native language. I believe that is a gross oversimplification especially given the rate at which new technologies change and develop. In any classroom there will be a range of ICT fluency, just as there is a range of linguistic or mathematical ability.

If you want to plan the effective use of ICT in your teaching, a good case study to look at is 'Using ICT to address "hard to teach" concepts: English case study', which you can find on the DCSF Standards site.

You will notice that there is a very systematic and structured approach to the planning of this initiative, involving first of all the identification of 'hard to teach' concepts in English. This review involved reviewing a range of reports, asking teachers themselves, and asking pupils. The three areas selected from this to focus on were:

- planning for writing;
- authorial view in reading;
- sentence structure in writing.

Follow through some of the links from this home page, and you will see the care which was given to the use of some very simple technology to develop effective teaching and learning strategies. It is interesting, and perhaps instructive, to note that these explorations start from asking questions about teaching and learning, not about ICT. Sound learning outcomes were identified, and then appropriate ICT approaches selected in order the help pupils achieve these outcomes.

A range of case studies relating to curriculum initiatives, including ICT, can be found on the national strategies site, **http://nationalstrategies.standards.dcsf.gov.uk**

Stop and Read

You can find a range of other case studies on the use of ICT on the DCSF standards site.

Dean, J. (2009) *Organising Learning in the Primary School Classroom* (4th edn). Abingdon: Routledge
Chapter 12 of this book deals with the use of ICT in the primary classroom, suggests other texts that you might consult, and raises some practice-based questions for teachers reviewing the use of ICT in their own practice.

Wergerif, R. and Dawes, L. (2004) *Thinking and Learning with ICT: Raising achievement in primary classrooms*. Abingdon, New York: RoutledgeFalmer.
This highly engaging book suggests that teachers can help ensure the effectiveness of computer-based activities by making sure that:

- learning dialogues are fostered in classrooms;
- software and applications are chosen which support learning dialogues with a focus on curriculum learning;
- activities are created that necessitate learning dialogues.

If you only read one part of this book, read Chapter 5 on the use of Bubble Dialogue and follow up by visiting this site: **www.dialogbox.org.uk/index.htm**

Woollard, J. (2007) *Learning and Teaching Using ICT*. Exeter: Learning Matters.
This book, although primarily addressed to trainee teachers continues to be useful to qualified teachers in that it provides ideas for and pointers to resources, raises many questions that will challenge your own thinking as a teacher and user of ICT, and supplies a range of ideas for the subject-based use of ICT.

Case Study

The changing 14–19 agenda

This case study presents an account of teachers developing their practice in a changing environment, as they take account of new national initiatives. When you read this case study, look in particular at the ways in which Dev and Angela need to learn more about each other's professional contexts and the external drivers in each, the ways in which ongoing collaboration across the different sectors enriched their enquiry by bringing alternative perspectives, and the ways in which they also had the capacity to develop their practice in relation to leadership development.

Dev is an early-career geography teacher, and has been in post for just over a year. The department he works in is planning to collaborate with the local college in teaching the BTEC First Diploma in Travel and Tourism. Although initially designed for post-16 pupils, as in many schools and colleges, this qualification is now being used to supplement the Key Stage 4 curriculum and offered in place of other GCSE options. It is equivalent to four GCSEs, and as such, represents a significant investment for everyone concerned. When the new diploma qualifications are introduced they want to be well placed to offer this to students. Dev has been given the job of liaising with Angela, the local college tutor, herself relatively new to teaching. Angela teaches these students on Tuesday afternoons when they attend the college. Both Dev and Angela have been acknowledged by their tutors and mentors, and now their more senior colleagues, as good teachers, who plan well, teach effectively and have good relationships with pupils.

As part of the diploma, Dev brings along twelve 14-year-old students (1 boy and 11 girls) every Tuesday afternoon for a three-hour teaching session. It is important to Dev and the school that this collaboration works, as it will provide a mechanism for improving the chances of these students to attain five A*–C GCSE qualifications

Four weeks into the programme, some issues start arising.

- The students seem uninterested in the college sessions and are very easily distracted.
- They have already missed one session because of an open day at school and will not be attending the following week due to a school exam.
- Angela finds the behaviour of the students is not consistent with that of her existing students, who are all over 16, and she is unsure of how to adjust her teaching to accommodate this.
- Dev is concerned that these issues might cause the programme to be less successful than it should be, and is also aware of plans to introduce the New Specialist Diploma in 2010 which will require precisely this sort of collaboration.

Reflecting on new initiatives

In the case study above Dev and Angela arranged a two-hour reflection meeting, so that they could assess the situation to date. They considered the underlying reasons for some of the issues which had arisen, and felt that they fitted into the following categories.

Preparation of students for college
Dev realised that the students were very unprepared for college. The environment was both physically and culturally different to that of schools, and teaching strategies were unfamiliar. The students seemed to think that college would be a more 'grown-up' and possibly liberal environment, and that normal school rules and expectations would be relaxed.

Preparation of themselves for the collaboration
They both realised that they had not fully understood the implications of this type of collaboration, and that they had not prepared themselves as well for it as they might have. Dev realised that he had not prepared the students well for the expectations that would be placed upon them, and Angela realised that she had not anticipated that teaching 14-year-olds would be so different. Both realised that they were quite unfamiliar with the other's world of work, and the procedures and protocols within it.

School–college negotiations
It was also realised that things outside the immediate control of either Dev or Angela were highly important. If it was not possible for them to reschedule events like open days and examinations, then these dates needed to be identified at the outset, and factored in to the collaborative planning. Neither had realised that the other sector would have this type of demands and constraints.

Both Dev and Angela felt that in exploring and identifying some of these issues and causes, they had provided a starting point for significant professional development. Angela was able to share the planning of her teaching and subsequent reflections with Dev, which in turn gave him an opportunity to explore and challenge his own approach to teaching. In sharing their planning, and later reflections and evaluations, they both found that their subject knowledge and their pedagogy were developed. They also gained important insights into the challenges and benefits of working collaboratively. A further benefit to both was the opportunity they had to explore concepts of emerging leadership capacity. Each of them was able to take a lead role in staff development sessions on collaborative working, and was able to lead and inform planning on similar collaborative provision.

Action Point

What do you think might be a cause of some of the issues here? What do you think Dev can do to address some of these issues? How might he find out why the students seem so unsettled and so easily distracted? What do you think Angela might do? How do you think they might work together, and with the support of both the school and college, support both of them through this new way of working?

Stop and Read

Hodgson, A. and Spours, K. (2008) *Education & Training 14–19: Curriculum, Qualifications and Organisation*. London: Sage.

This text gives a clear history of developments in recent years in 14–19 education and considers the specialist diplomas and their introduction and the impact on schools and colleges.

Vizard, D. (2007) *How to Manage Behaviour in Further Education*. London: Paul Chapman Publishing.

This text looks at managing behaviour and considers the issues surrounding 14–16-year-olds as well as traditional 16–19-year-olds in further education.

Strategies for developing this content area

This chapter is, as indicated at the start, broad in scope, and as such, provides a rich seam of assessment opportunities.

You will have seen in the first part of this chapter how teachers in different situations used a range of strategies in developing their practice in relation to content area 2.

In summary, these strategies were as follows.

Working with mentors and more experienced colleagues

This will be a key aspect of your ongoing professional development in your early years as a teacher. Indeed, working with colleagues, sharing with and learning from each other is part and parcel of every teacher's professional practice. During your MTL, your school-based coaches and mentors will provide you with opportunities to develop many aspects of your practice, while your tutor will help you address these opportunities in a way that allows you to meet master's-level learning outcomes.

Working with specialist support, such as a subject association or an LA consultant

You will find this an important aspect of your ongoing professional development. Educational syllabi are not static, and frameworks for qualifications change. LA consultants are in place to provide the specialist support needed as you learn your craft as a teacher, and to assist teachers in times of change and development.

Working in collaborative peer groups

For many years, teaching was a relatively isolated profession. What happened in the class-room was between the teacher and the pupils, and unless school inspectors were visiting, it was unusual for any teacher to have another adult in their classroom while they were teaching. However, it is now the case that it is more unusual to have the teacher as the only adult in the classroom. This change in practice, and other developments in teacher initial and continuing education, have encouraged a more collaborative approach to the planning, carrying out and evaluating of teaching. Throughout your career, you will find that the benefits of well-planned collaborations are manifold.

Focused, independent research

As a professional, you are expected to take responsibility for your own learning and professional development. Specifically, as part of the professional standards, you are required to evaluate your own performance, and have a creative and constructively critical approach towards innovation, being prepared to adapt practice where benefits and improvements are identified.

Different perspectives

Collaboration with other professionals, or other teachers who work in a different sector to yourself, will often bring fresh perspectives to your work. Their naïve questions may often challenge you to explore those things that you have taken for granted in your own practice without ever having explored underlying assumptions.

You should have opportunities to use strategies like these at all stages in your career as a teacher, but more especially in your early years of teaching. There are obviously other ways in which you can improve your subject, pedagogy and curriculum development. For many teachers attending INSET courses with LA or other providers, where they are available, is a valuable way of enhancing their professional skills. In its 2007 publication, *Making CPD Better*, the GTC states that:

> *Effective CPD maintains a clear focus on pupils' learning. It is grounded in what is known about effective adult learning.*
> *This includes:*
>
> * *sustained access to coaching and mentoring, for getting support with knowledge and/or skills;*
> * *opportunities to see good practice in action, both in classrooms and in adult learning environments;*
> * *a range of opportunities for observation and feedback as part of collaborative and collegial working practices; and*
> * *sustained, structured and cumulative opportunities for practising and evaluating what has been learnt.*

Teachers have also found postgraduate study a useful opportunity, particularly in the way in which it provides a framework and support for critical reflection on practice, and opportunities to implement and evaluate interventions. Your MTL has been structured to build on opportunities like these, so that you can personalise your own learning needs within your own professional context.

In the second part of the chapter, you saw how Angela and Dev both improved their knowledge of each other's settings and curricula, while at the same time enhancing their own professional practice.

If you are a primary school teacher, the Primary Framework provides many opportunities for you to work with colleagues in a developmental way which will enhance your professional knowledge and experience. Schools are urged to consider six key areas as they implement the Framework.

1. Improving the teaching of early reading.
2. Encouraging flexibility.
3. Structuring learning.
4. Raising expectations.
5. Making more effective use of assessment.
6. Broadening and strengthening pedagogy.

Working closely with other colleagues, you should take opportunities to be involved in the discussions around these areas, and the planning required to address them. For each of these themes, there are possible actions you could take. These actions, as well as having a direct impact on your practice, could also usefully form the basis of tasks or assignments for your MTL.

Assignments

Suggested assignments to address this content area
When you undertake your MTL, you will be encouraged to engage in school-based practice development work which can be the basis for assignments/assessment opportunities for MTL modules. The following list may provide some useful prompts within this content area.

- Consider some aspect of your teaching, perhaps a key concept in primary mathematics learning, or some aspect of your secondary subject area, and explore ways in which you have reviewed your practice, and made attempts to improve it through improving your subject knowledge and pedagogy. Put together a portfolio of evidence, structured in three sections.
    1. Introduction to the study, including a rationale for undertaking it.
    2. Evidence from what you have done.
    3. Evaluation of what you have done.
- Reflect on the relationship you have with your tutor and mentor, and explore the impact that this triadic partnership has had on your professional learning. Use notes from your meetings, and reflections on them to prepare an assignment on how this relationship has helped you develop your understanding of curriculum and curriculum changes and developments.
- If you have the opportunity to work as a collaborative group with colleagues on MTL, conduct a mutual assessment of your strengths and areas for development, and on the basis of this, draw up, implement and evaluate an action plan to support your development in identified areas.

Table 4.2 Implementing the framework

Area	Your actions
Improving the teaching of early reading	• Familiarise yourself with the (2006) Rose Review (Review of Early Reading), and work with a colleague to develop some resources for the teaching of phonics and early reading • Design and teach a lesson to develop children's speaking and listening skills. Reflect on your teaching, assessing the impact you are having on reading development for your pupils
Encouraging flexibility	• Work with colleagues to assess pupils' learning and future needs and on the basis of this design a number of lessons with different structures, showing how their design is appropriate for the learning needs of the pupils • If you have the opportunity to work with some pupils who have special educational needs, are gifted and talented, or who have English as an additional language, plan some lessons to meet their specific needs. Ask a colleague to act as a critical friend and review the teaching of these lessons with you
Structuring learning	• Work with the literacy co-ordinator on the planning of a 2- or 4-week unit of work • Work with the mathematics or numeracy coordinator on the planning of a 2- or 4-week unit of work • Develop skills in independently planning a unit of work, identifying objectives and cycles of review, teach, practise, apply and evaluate over each unit
Raising expectations	• Review the learning objectives in a set of Year 3 or Year 4 mathematics lessons, and develop a revised set of objectives, which provide more pace • Review a set of lesson plans in Years 5 or 6, and identify opportunities to consolidate the learning from earlier years • Involve pupils in setting learning targets, and develop some lessons on this basis
Making more effective use of assessment	• Work closely with more experienced colleagues in order to improve your assessment for learning skills • Keep a record of pupil progress during lessons, and across a unit of work. Reflect on and review your own teaching as a result of this
Broadening and strengthening pedagogy	• Start thinking and reading about pedagogical approaches. Find out about exploratory pedagogical approaches, and select a topic for which it would be appropriate, and develop a set of lessons. Write a reflective commentary on the process

- Whether you teach in the primary or the secondary sector, identify one aspect of your teaching that you could approach mainly through the use of ICT. Identify the key concepts you want to develop, and suggest a specific ICT approach (software or application) which you will use. Explain the pedagogic justification for your choice.
- Consider one of the new developments appropriate to your own practice, and discuss the implications of its introduction on you and your colleagues in terms of both pedagogy and management.
- Consider one of the new developments appropriate to your own practice, and discuss the implications of its introduction on pupils in terms of their learning experience.
- Visit the Becta website. Find out what resources are available for you in your subject, or age range, and having discussed this with colleagues or your mentor, select one and evaluate it in terms of how it enhances pedagogy.
- If your department has not yet introduced a diploma, work with a colleague and construct an outline plan for its introduction. Suggest appropriate professional development that you and your colleagues would require in order to support this implementation.
- If your department has already introduced a diploma, discuss with the head of the department and other colleagues the impact this has had on their teaching (in terms of subject knowledge and pedagogy), and the impact it has had on pupil learning in terms of motivation and achievement.

Summary

At the end of this chapter you should have:
- **devised strategies for supporting your own subject knowledge development;**
- **worked with peers, colleagues and/or mentors to explore ways in which to improve pedagogy in your subject or phase;**
- **developed your awareness of subject associations, and their value in supporting your subject knowledge development;**
- **considered the creative use of ICT in a pedagogically justified way in an aspect of your teaching;**
- **become familiar with the range of developments in your own subject and/or phase.**

Further reading

Boys, R. and Spink, E. (2008) *Primary Curriculum: Teaching the core subjects*. London: Continuum.

Briggs, A. and Sommerfeldt, D. (2002) *Managing Effective Learning and Teaching*. London: Paul Chapman Publishing.

Dillon, J. and Maguire, M. (eds) (2007) *Becoming a Teacher: Issues in secondary teaching*.

Maidenhead: Open University Press/McGraw-Hill.

Kalmbach Phillips, D. and Carr, K. (2006) *Becoming a Teacher Through Action Research*. New York: Routledge.

Loughran, J. (2006) *Developing a Pedagogy of Teacher Education*. Abingdon: Routledge.

Overall, L. and Sangster, M. (2007) *Secondary Teacher's Handbook*. London: Continuum International.

Webb, R. (ed.) (2006) *Changing Teaching and Learning in the Primary School*. Maidenhead: Open University Press/McGraw-Hill.

Useful websites

Becta **www.becta.org.uk**

The Department for Children, Schools and Families **www.dcsf.gov.uk**

The National Strategies **www.nationalstrategies.standards.dcsf.gov.uk**

The Council for Subject Associations **www.subjectassociations.org.uk**

Teachernet **www.teachernet.gov.uk**

The Diploma Directgov site **http://yp.direct.gov.uk/diplomas/**

CHAPTER 5

Content area 3: Child development, inclusion and behaviour

We know nothing of childhood: and with our mistaken notions the further we advance the further we go astray.

(Rousseau in the Preface to *Émile*)

Chapter Objectives

By the end of this chapter, you should have:
- an awareness of the complexity of child development;
- an understanding of self-concept, relationships and teacher–student attachment;
- an understanding of the literature, research and legislation surrounding the inclusion of students described as having behavioural difficulties;
- an awareness of the values, attitudes, principles and practicalities of inclusion for individuals designated as having behavioural, emotional and social difficulties (BESD);
- an understanding of your own beliefs and your position in the inclusion debate;
- been enabled to take the thinking that you have started to do around self-concept and relationships and use it to develop your understanding of the theories and dilemmas associated with inclusion as a concept;
- examined the behaviours of all members of the school community in order to understand structural, cultural and attitudinal barriers to inclusion.

Links to the professional standards

This part of your MTL will address the following core standards. Appendix 1 will show you a table illustrating how you can progress from core to the higher standards through addressing this content area.

Professional attributes

Q1, Q2, Q4, Q5, Q7

> **Professional knowledge and understanding**
> Q10, Q18, Q19, Q21
>
> **Professional skills**
> Q31

This chapter aims to introduce you to the complex worlds of child development, inclusion and behaviour. The first section of the chapter deals specifically with childhood and child development, and frames these concepts in a way which leads us, as professionals, to explore and challenge our own thinking around how we understand and relate to children and young people.

The second section brings us from concepts of childhood and child development to professional overviews, theoretical perspectives and legislation in relation to inclusive education. The concept of inclusion and behaviour is then introduced and discussed in depth. Throughout, you will be encouraged to reflect on your own practice in relation to what you are reading. I will then introduce you to two short case studies about a young student, J, who challenged my thinking in terms of inclusion, child development and behaviour. You are encouraged to use the technique of critical incident capture and analysis to explore and challenge your own thinking and assumptions.

These fields demand a lifetime of study and it is hoped that your MTL is the beginning of many years of professional reflection, reading and thinking. Thus, you should expect, at the end of this chapter, to have more questions than answers and to feel more unsettled than certain. If I can achieve one thing, it will be to encourage you to embrace uncertainty and to open your mind to new ways of thinking about teaching and learning.

Section 1: Child development, inclusion and behaviour

Introduction
The concept of child development is, necessarily, an adult construct through which childhood is made intelligible, both in the everyday world, and within the specialist vocabularies of the education professionals charged with the responsibility of 'development'. However, before we begin to consider theories of development, it is essential that we spend some time considering childhood.

Reflection

What do you bring to mind when you contemplate childhood?
• Do you think of yourself or of another?

- Who are you when you contemplate childhood? An educator? A parent? A former child? A member of society?

Even the briefest of considerations of these questions highlight the complexity of this field. We can, however, begin the journey.

There are many ways in which we could approach child development. For some, consideration of cognitive, emotional and psychological development would be a natural starting point. For others, areas of development, whether they be communication and interaction, cognition and learning, behavioural, emotional and social or physical and sensory, would be an equally important starting point. In a chapter of this nature, that intends to consider child development in terms of inclusion and behaviour, the chosen starting point is to consider child development in terms of self-concept and relationships. This is not to ignore wider theoretical perspectives, merely to make this chapter a basis for further reading.

Self-concept, self-esteem and relationships

Self-concept or self-identity is the mental and conceptual awareness and persistent regard that people hold with respect to their own being.

Components of a being's self-concept include physical, psychological and social attributes, and can be influenced by the person's attitudes, habits, beliefs and ideas. These components and attributes can each be related to the general concepts of self-image and self-esteem.

One of the most influential voices in self-concept theory was that of Carl Rogers (1947), who introduced an entire theoretical system built around the importance of the self. In Rogers's view, the self is the central ingredient in human personality and personal adjustment. Rogers described the self as a social product, developing out of interpersonal relationships and striving for consistency. He maintained that there is a basic human need for positive regard both from others and from oneself. He also believed that in every person there is a tendency towards self-actualisation and development so long as this is permitted and encouraged by the immediate environment.

Self-esteem or self-worth, on the other hand, includes a person's subjective appraisal of himself or herself as intrinsically positive or negative to some degree.

Self-esteem involves both self-relevant beliefs (e.g. 'I am competent/incompetent', 'I am liked/disliked') and associated self-relevant emotions (e.g. pride/shame, triumph/despair). It also finds expression in behaviour (e.g. confidence/caution, assertiveness/passivity). In addition, self-esteem can be construed as an enduring personality characteristic (trait self-esteem) or as a temporary psychological condition (state self-esteem). Finally, self-esteem can be specific to a particular dimension (e.g. 'I believe I am a good writer, and feel proud of that in particular') or global in extent (e.g. 'I believe I am a good person, and feel proud of myself in general').

One of the strongest theoretical influences on the study of relationships is attachment theory, particularly the work of Bowlby (1907–90). Much that has been written about attachment focuses on the child–parent relationship; however, some authors have specifically considered child–teacher relationships in terms of attachment. Howes and Ritchie (2002) introduce their thinking around child–teacher relationships with the following:

> *According to attachment theory, in which we ground our approach to the development of trusting relationships between children and teachers (Bowlby, 1982), all children become attached to their important adult caregivers, including teachers. Furthermore, again according to this theory, every attachment relationship has an organization. Attachment theorists suggest that there are three basic attachment organizations: secure; avoidant insecure; and insecure ambivalent/resistant (Ainsworth, Blehar, Waters, and Wall, 1978). A fourth category, disorganized, describes relationships that are incoherent and fragmented. The optimal attachment organization is a secure one. When child–teacher attachment relationships are secure, children trust that they can get help from their teacher when they need it.*
>
> (Howes and Ritchie, 2002, p13)

Reflection

I have selected this particular text as it is easy to ascribe attachment difficulties to the parent–child relationship. What is more challenging, but nevertheless significant, is the realisation that the child–teacher relationship is equally crucial. Consider a child that you have been dealing with on a regular basis. How do you think the child relates to you, and trusts you? How can you ensure that your classroom provides the environment and climate for the formation of secure attachments? Do you think it should?

Stop and Read

The following texts offer interesting perspectives on relationships in the classroom.

Salmon, D. and Freedman, R. A. (2002) *Facilitating Interpersonal Relationships in the Classroom: The relational literacy curriculum.* Mahwah, NJ: Lawrence Erlbaum Associates.

Raider-Roth, M. and Gilligan, C. (2005) *Trusting What You Know: The high stakes of classroom relationships.* San Francisco, CA: Jossey-Bass.

Action Point

- Think about the classroom environment and list all of the behaviours that you might see, including those demonstrated by adults.
- Reflect upon what this list tells you about the self-concept of individual learners.
- Consider the ways in which relationships in the classroom contribute to the development of high, and low, self-esteem.

Section 2: Inclusion and behaviour

The most effective teaching for learners with the most difficult behaviour is little different to the most successful teaching for others.

(Ofsted, 2005, p15)

Concepts and theories of inclusion

Many teachers undertaking master's-level qualifications describe a profound sense of confusion when attempting to understand inclusion. The plethora of definitions and perspectives available can seem contradictory and this often leaves teachers feeling more confused than ever. It is necessary, therefore, to start this chapter with a brief scoping exercise around how the academic and professional worlds of education define inclusion.

Inclusion and inclusive education

Inclusion is generally understood around the world as part of a human rights agenda that demands access to, and equity in, society. However, such concepts are problematic in their interpretation: for example, there is much debate around what constitutes human rights and about the difference between access and equity. For the purposes of this chapter, we will examine just three of the many perspectives on inclusion and inclusive education. This is intended to be an introduction to the field rather than a précis of a complex area.

Inclusion as process

The Index for Inclusion (Booth and Ainscow, 2002) is one set of materials that aims to guide schools through a process of inclusive school development.

The Index takes the social model of disability as its starting point, based on the premise that people are not disabled because of a specific set of internal factors, but that, instead, they are disabled because of how society is constructed.

The Index argues that inclusive education involves the following.

- Valuing all students and staff equally.
- Increasing the participation of students in, and reducing their exclusion from, the cultures, curricula and communities of local schools.

- Restructuring the cultures, policies and practices in schools so that they respond to the diversity of students in the locality.
- Reducing barriers to learning and participation for all students, not only those with impairments or those who are categorised as 'having special educational needs'.
- Learning from attempts to overcome barriers to the access and participation of particular students to make changes for the benefit of students more widely.
- Viewing the difference between students as resources to support learning, rather than as problems to be overcome.
- Acknowledging the right of students to an education in their locality.
- Improving schools for staff as well as for students.
- Emphasising the role of schools in building community and developing values, as well as in increasing achievement.
- Fostering mutually sustaining relationships between schools and communities.
- Recognising that inclusion in education is one aspect of inclusion in society.

Inclusion as social justice

From a social justice perspective, inclusive education is concerned with the quest for equity, social justice and participation; it is about the removal of all forms of barriers of discrimination and oppression and it is about the well-being of all.

In 2002, Rustemeir authored a groundbreaking report published by the Centre for Studies in Inclusive Education (CSIE) entitled *Social and Educational Justice: The Human Rights Framework for Inclusion*. The report claims that the central problem in the development of inclusive education in the UK is the continuing philosophical, financial and legislative support of segregated schooling. In this report Rustemeir argues that segregation in separate special schools is internationally recognised as discriminatory and damaging to individuals and society and that as well as violating children's rights to inclusive education, segregated schooling breaches all four principles underpinning the 1989 UN Convention on the Rights of the Child. The report acknowledges progress in developing the capacity of mainstream schools in the UK to enable all children and young people to learn together, but stresses that special schools remain as a fundamental obstacle to inclusion.

In addition, Rustemeir expresses genuine concern that inclusion has come to mean almost everything but the elimination of exclusion and argues that philosophies grounded in social and educational justice challenge several widely held assumptions sustaining segregation. These include deeply held, unsubstantiated beliefs about the impossibility of ever including all children in mainstream, the supposedly 'huge expense' of full inclusion, and the so-called sanctity of parental choice. According to the author there are limits to parental choice, arguing that children's rights to inclusive education are universal – they apply to all children, everywhere, including those whose parents would prefer them to go to special schools.

Inclusion as 'philosophy of difference'

Allen (2008) writes eloquently about philosophies of difference stating that: *the spaces of schooling, teacher education and education policy and legislation, which are rigid striated and hierarchical, with clear lines of demarcation, produce exclusion* (2008, p55). She argues that:

> *Inclusion has been plagued by platitudes with regard to difference, in which teachers are urged to 'celebrate' diversity and difference. Apart from the absence of any indica- tion of how such celebrations might be done, the language itself is patronising ... The emergence of these empty, vacuous platitudes is associated with an inability to avoid the repetition of exclusion and the use of a complex system of pathologies to define, divide and treat difference. The inevitable and irresistible repetition of exclusion arises from a fear of difference and a need to control it or make sense of it and the teachers' unions have made it clear that some difference is more frightening for their members than others.*
>
> (Allen, 2008, p65)

In this seminal text, Allen uses the work of the French philosophers Deluze, Guattari, Derrida and Foucault to argue that philosophical ideas, rather than more practical guidance or solutions, are needed to revive the inclusion agenda.

Reflection

- What is your position in relation to these perspectives?
- How do you live your beliefs in the classroom?
- What are the barriers to this way of working and how can you overcome these?

Legislation relating to inclusive education

There are national and international laws that seek to address discrimination in education and support inclusive education in the UK. What follows is a brief summary of the legislative landscape.

The Inclusion Charter (Centre for Studies in Inclusive Education, CSIE, 1989)

The Inclusion Charter was the first document in the United Kingdom (UK) to put inclusive education, and the ending of segregation, on the human rights platform.

The Education Act 1996

Part IV of the Education Act was concerned specifically with Special Educational Needs and was revised in 2001 and is now an Act on its own, the Special Educational Needs and Disability Act (SENDA, 2001); see below.

Excellence for All Children (1997)

This consultation document supported the 1994 Salamanca Statement (see below). In this context the Green Paper posited the *progressive extension of the capacity of mainstream schools to provide for children with a wide range of needs*. However, alongside this move towards inclusion the government made it clear that special schools still had a role to play in an inclusive education system.

Inclusive Schooling (DfES, 2001)

This document provided statutory guidance on the practical operation of the new framework for inclusion of children with special educational needs into mainstream schools. The advice given in this guidance document covered: how the statutory framework for inclusion and provisions within the Education Act 1996 apply to children and examples of the sort of steps maintained schools should consider taking to ensure that a child's inclusion is not incompatible with the efficient education of other children.

Special Educational Needs and Disability Act (SENDA, 2001)

This Act states that it will be unlawful for responsible bodies to treat a disabled person 'less favourably' than a non-disabled person for a reason that relates to the person's disability.

If a disabled person is at a 'substantial disadvantage', responsible bodies are required to take reasonable steps to prevent that disadvantage. This might include:

- changes to policies and practices;
- changes to course requirements or work placements;
- changes to the physical features of a building;
- the provision of interpreters or other support workers;
- the delivery of courses in alternative ways;
- the provision of material in other formats.

Every Child Matters (ECM, 2003)

This Green Paper aimed to create a joined-up system of health, family support, childcare and education services so that all children get the best start possible. It was hoped that through the range of measures brought in under the Every Child Matters: Change for Children programme, organisations providing services to children, such as schools, hospitals and the police, would be enabled to work together and share information, so that all children, and especially those from vulnerable groups, have the support they need to:

- be healthy;
- stay safe;
- enjoy and achieve;
- make a positive contribution;
- achieve economic well-being.

Children Act 2004

The Children Act sought to provide the legislative spine for the Every Child Matters: Change for Children programme, in order to drive the local and national changes to the system of children's services that are needed to deliver:

- improved outcomes for children and young people;
- a focus on opportunities for all and narrowing gaps;
- support for parents, carers and families;
- a shift to prevention, early identification and intervention;
- integrated and personalised services;
- better safeguards for children and young people.

Removing Barriers to Achievement (2004)

This strategy sets out the government's vision for enabling children with special educational needs to realise their potential and includes a programme of sustained action and review over a number of years to support Early Years settings, schools and local authorities in improving provision for children with SEN.

This vision is articulated around four themes.

1. Early intervention.
2. Removing barriers to learning.
3. Raising expectations and achievement.
4. Delivering improvements in partnership.

Disability Discrimination Act (DDA, 2005)

This Act introduced new duties for most public bodies to:

- promote disability equality;
- take steps to eliminate discrimination and harassment;
- publish a Disability Equality Scheme, setting out how they plan to achieve these aims.

The aim is to influence the way public bodies – including education providers – make decisions and develop their policies, encouraging them to consider the needs of disabled people as part of their everyday activities.

Select Committee report (2006)

This report urged the Government to clarify its position on SEN – specifically on inclusion – and to provide national strategic direction for the future. The report stated that *The Government needs to provide a clear over-arching strategy for SEN and disability policy. It needs to provide a vision for the future that everyone involved in SEN can purposefully work towards. The Government should be up-front about its change of direction on SEN policy and the inclusion agenda, if this is indeed the case, and should reflect this in updated statutory and non-statutory guidance to the sector.*

The Education and Inspections Act 2006
This Act introduced a duty on schools to promote community cohesion, with effect from September 2007.

In addition, the UK has ratified the following international human rights treaties which place the Government under an obligation to provide education free from discrimination.

UNESCO Convention Against Discrimination in Education (1960)
This Convention addresses many aspects of discrimination in education. It covers the issues of separate schools based on language, gender and religion, and of private schools. It is also a cornerstone of UNESCO's 'Education for All' movement.

UN Convention on the Rights of the Child (ratified by the UK in 1991)
This convention is built around four general principles: non-discrimination, the best interests of the child, optimal development and the voice of the child.

In June 1994 representatives of 92 governments and 25 international organisations formed the World Conference on Special Needs Education, held in Salamanca, Spain. They agreed a dynamic new statement on the education of all disabled children, which called for inclusion to be the norm.

UNESCO: Inclusive Education on the Agenda (1998)
This paper summarised the longstanding background to discrimination against marginalised children and young people arguing that: *In most, if not all, countries disadvantaged children and young people remain excluded from, or marginalised within, the education systems.*

In March 2007, the UK signed the UN Convention on the Rights of Persons with Disabilities. The right to inclusive education is enshrined in article 24 of this convention, which states:

> *Parties shall ensure an inclusive education system at all levels and lifelong learning directed to:*
> a. *the full development of human potential and sense of dignity and self-worth, and the strengthening of respect for human rights, fundamental freedoms and human diversity;*
> b. *the development by persons with disabilities of their personality, talents and creativity, as well as their mental and physical abilities, to their fullest potential;*
> c. *enabling persons with disabilities to participate effectively in a free society.*

Reflection

- How many of these pieces of legislation were you previously aware of?
- Are these legislative imperatives evident in the classroom? If so, how; if not, why not?
- How do you interpret the term 'disability' (for example, as it is used in SENDA or the DDA)?
- Do you think that 'disability' is a positive term? Why? Why not?

Inclusion and behaviour

In order to examine the thorny issue of inclusion and behaviour, a number of opportunities for reflection have been designed in order to enable your critical engagement with the issues highlighted thus far in relation to behaviour. As the young person identified in the case studies is described as experiencing behavioural, emotional and social difficulties (BESD), it is important that we examine this in a little detail before examining the case studies and critical incidents.

Concepts and theories of BESD

As human behaviour is an area that we all have experience of, it can be tempting to believe that we understand behaviour even before we have considered a range of theoretical perspectives. Indeed, all too often, attempts to understand and deal with behavioural difficulties in schools tend to focus on the pupil as being, and having, the problem.

Therefore, as before, for the purposes of this chapter, we will examine just three of the many perspectives on BESD. Once again, this is intended to be an introduction to the field rather than a précis of a complex area.

Behaviourism

Cooper (1994, p31) offers a useful description of behaviourism as:

> *The key concept is the notion that all behaviour, including unacceptable behaviour, occurs because it is reinforced. Thus, in relation to a behavioural difficulty in school, it is necessary to examine the classroom environment and the behaviour of the teachers and other pupils, to determine how that behaviour is being reinforced. This is never easy, and the suggestion that teachers may reinforce unacceptable behaviour patterns is one that many teachers find difficult to accept. Yet teachers, even those in special schools and units, spend a large proportion of their time dealing with misbehaviour and a relatively small proportion of their time focusing on good behaviour. While the 'dealing with bad behaviour' might be done unpleasantly, with the intention of stopping it, or tolerantly, in order to communicate an understanding of the child's distress, the attention gained during these interactions can be reinforcing and, paradoxically, strengthen the very behaviour that it is intended to eliminate. Implicit in this position is*

the assertion that it is possible to change behaviour by manipulating the consequences of the behaviour or changing the situation in which it occurs.

Humanism

The humanistic approach was developed in the 1950s by Rogers, among others, who felt that existing theories failed to adequately address the meaning of behaviour, and the nature of healthy growth.

There are several factors which distinguish the humanistic approach from other approaches, including the emphasis on subjective meaning, a rejection of determinism, and a concern for positive growth rather than pathology. Some theorists believe that behaviour can only be understood objectively (by an impartial observer), but humanists argue that this results in concluding that an individual is incapable of understanding their own behaviour – a view which they see as both paradoxical and dangerous to well-being. Instead, Rogers argues that the meaning of behaviour is essentially personal and subjective.

In terms of his theory, there are two fundamental ideas which are particularly worth noting.

Firstly, Rogers talked about healthy development in terms of how the individual perceives their own being. A healthy individual will tend to see congruence between their sense of who they are (self) and who they feel they should be (ideal self). While no one tends to experience perfect congruence at all times, the relative degree of congruence is an indicator of health.

The second fundamental idea is Rogers's concept of the conditions for healthy growth. Through a process Rogers called person-centred approaches, the therapist (or teacher) seeks to provide empathy, openness, and unconditional positive regard. Lack of these conditions, a humanist would argue, leads to behavioural, emotional and social difficulties.

Ecosystemic perspective

Papatheodorou (2005, p35) describes ecosystemic ways of understanding behaviour as:

> *In ecosystemic terms children and their behaviour cannot meaningfully be seen in isolation from their contexts. Behaviour is seen as the result of the dynamic interrelationships and interactions between personal and environmental variables, between, and within, different systems where the child finds him/herself... The ecosystemic approach assumes that there is no linear cause and effect for a problem, but that behaviour is maintained by the total interaction and not just by reinforcement... For example, a young person's behaviour may be the result of the interactions with the other young people or adults, or because of the layout of the room... The introduction of the ecosystemic approach was an important step in understanding the complexities of human behaviour, since instead of employing an inside-out dichotomy, it emphasises the study of interrelationships between and within systems which affect behaviour. The causes of any instances of problem behaviour are part of a complex formation of actions and reactions between the participants.*

Reflection

- How would a behaviourist, humanist or ecosystemic educator respond to confrontational behaviour?
- Which of these theoretical approaches is closest to your own beliefs about behaviour?

Legislation relating to behaviour

You need to be familiar with contemporary legislation in this respect. The following list provides a brief overview.

Managing Challenging Behaviour (Ofsted Report, 2005)

This report found the following.

- The most common form of poor behaviour is consistent low-level disruption of lessons that wears down staff and interrupts learning.
- A strong sense of community and positive engagement with parents are features of schools where behaviour is good.
- A significant proportion of pupils with difficult behaviour have SEN and face disadvantage and disturbance in their family lives.
- A strong lead by senior managers who set high standards and provide close support for staff contributes significantly to the effective management of behaviour.

Learning Behaviour (Steer Report, 2005)

Three recommendations of the Steer Report were as follows.

1. Respect has to be given in order to be received. Parents and carers, pupils and teachers all have to operate in a culture of mutual regard.
2. Schools should review their learning, teaching and behaviour policies and undertake a behaviour audit (2005, p11).
3. We believe that no school policy is of any value if it is not understood and applied consistently by all staff (2005, p13).

Education and Inspection Act 2006

This Act provided schools with:

- the legal right to confiscate inappropriate items from pupils such as mobile phones or music players;
- statutory powers to discipline pupils who behave badly on the way to and from school, for instance when travelling on buses and trains;

- greater legal scope and flexibility in giving pupils detentions, which may include after-school and Saturday detentions.

It also placed a legal duty on schools to make provision to tackle all forms of bullying.

Violent Crime Reduction Act 2006
This act introduced two important powers from May 2007.

1. Head teachers are allowed to search groups of pupils if they suspect one of them is carrying a knife.
2. Heads are also entitled to use metal-detector arches and wands to carry out random, non-intrusive searches of pupils for weapons.

Improving Behaviour (Ofsted, 2006)
This report stated that the schools that made the best progress:

- tackled the improvement of behaviour as part of a whole-school improvement programme;
- sought students' views about each stage of the improvement process, involved students in the improvement strategies and actively celebrated students behaving well;
- ensured that staff knew what to do when faced with unacceptable behaviour.

Revised guidance on the education of children and young people with behavioural, emotional and social difficulties (May 2008)
This guidance seeks to remind schools, Early Years settings and local authorities of existing advice on improving outcomes for these children through:

- whole-school promotion of positive behaviour;
- whole-school promotion of mental health;
- the application of principles and processes contained in the SEN Code of Practice alongside guidance set out in School Discipline and Pupil Behaviour Policies;
- the application of the Disability Discrimination Acts 1995 and 2005.

Reflection

What do these pieces of legislation tell us about our educational system?
How might each of these pieces of legislation impact upon learning environments?

Case studies

The following case studies chart the experiences of a child described as exhibiting behavioural difficulties. This child demonstrates behaviours described by The Steer and Ofsted Reports discussed earlier. As such, these case studies reflect the lived experiences of many children and young people in our education system. The case studies are not age-specific, they could relate as easily to a child in the Foundation stage as a student in further education.

Case Study

In the beginning

J doesn't have any particular friends at school, and when he is brought to school, either by parents or a social worker, he refuses to enter a classroom and sits in the entrance hall.

J is neither confrontational nor aggressive. When any members of staff try to engage him in conversation his answers are monosyllabic. He refuses to discuss why he won't engage in the school process, resorting to shrugging his shoulders when asked any questions about his conduct.

Critical incident

J does not have a physical education (PE) kit and one is loaned to him by his class teacher who stresses the importance of responsibility and trust and makes it clear that the PE kit must be returned, laundered, as soon as possible.

The next day the school is informed that a police raid had taken place on the home and that J's little sister had run away. The police inform the school that J had gone after her, in nothing but his boxer shorts, and brought her back to the family home an hour later.

J did not arrive in school that morning, with the taxi driver reporting that he couldn't get an answer at the house.

At 11 a.m., J arrived in school with the laundered PE kit. He explained that they had all overslept and that he had walked the four miles to school to return the PE kit. He had washed it himself.

Reflection

When you started to read the case study above, did you immediately draw a mental picture of the child? I suspect that most people did and that this picture is based upon negative experiences that we might have had or on the media portrayal of such families. Were you surprised that J walked the four-mile journey to school to return the PE kit and maintain trust? I was. I was the class teacher in this case and J taught me so much about the assumptions and prejudices that I unwittingly held. Cole (2005) offers some insights into such incidents by arguing that:

> *Missed schooling or social and emotional upsets are likely to be combined to make young people acutely aware of their recurrent failure in front of their peers.*
>
> (Cole, 2005, p162)

Given that this was undoubtedly the case in this instance, how much more difficult must it have been for J to walk into school late in order to maintain a trusting relationship with his class teacher? More importantly, what is the most appropriate response to this?

Stop and Read

In order to frame your thinking about this case study you might find the EPPI report, produced by the Evidence for Policy and Practice Information and Co-ordinating Centre (EPPI-Centre), a good starting point.

Powell, S. and Tod, J. (2004) A systematic review of how theories explain learning behaviour in school contexts. In *Research Evidence in Education Library*. London: EPPI-Centre, Social Science Research Unit, Institute of Education, University of London.

The report summarised key points as follows.

- Learning behaviour is influenced by the interaction of how the learner thinks, feels and interacts.
- Many of the learning behaviours studied were related to staying on-task in group settings and useful strategies related to the development of motivation and discipline, social behaviour and self-efficacy.
- Behaviour management could be improved by: promoting mastery orientation rather than performance orientation; promoting on-task discussion between pupils; working in partnership with pupils in goal setting; discouraging competitive classroom contexts.
- Positive learning behaviour can be enhanced by: emphasising effective learning behaviour through subject teaching; use of cognitive and affective strategies; formative assessment of social, emotional and behavioural indicators of learning; developing a shared understanding of learning behaviour between teacher and pupil; and increasing the integration of the 'social' and the 'academic'.

Action Point

Begin to capture 'critical incidents' in your own practice.

For me, a critical incident is one that challenges your own assumptions or makes you think differently about behaviour rather than one that demonstrates challenging behaviour on the part of the student.

Case Study

Three years later

J now has a history of chronic non-attendance. He is known to the police and social services and has the unwelcome notoriety of being the youngest boy in the authority to get an Anti-Social Behaviour Order (ASBO).

J has been at secondary school for almost two years but has not attended for over three months. He is currently on a 'two day a week' programme to attempt to reintroduce him to school. He communicates little with any staff members or other students and does not seem to be interested in any aspect of school life. When he arrives, he will go to class but will sit silently, refusing to work. At break time or lunchtime he leaves the premises and returns home.

Critical incident

Staff members visit J at home in an attempt to re-engage him. They talk about the Christmas production and the proposed holiday to the Lake District but point out that these aspects of school life are part of a bigger picture and can only be accessed with proper attendance. J's mum begs him to attend and promises some spending money for Christmas if he does so. J agrees to attend but, the following day, the taxi driver refuses to transport J and he gets out. The next day J refuses to travel in the taxi as he says that the driver doesn't like him.

Reflection

It is, perhaps, easy in this instance to wash our hands of such students: we have done all that we can; we have other learners to worry about. However, I can't help but reflect that in J's position, I cannot guarantee that I would behave any differently. Would I want someone to refuse to give up on me? It is often difficult to put ourselves in the shoes of others; to imagine their lifeworld when we have so many challenges of our own but, I would suggest that when we take a moment to do so, we become better teachers for all children.

Stop and Read

The following journal articles should help you to understand this incident from another perspective.

Turner, C. (2000) A pupil with emotional and behavioural difficulties perspective: does John feel that his behaviour is affecting his learning? *Emotional and Behavioural Difficulties*, 5 (4).
  This paper is written from the perspective of a Year 9 pupil with emotional and behavioural difficulties. The article indicates that the primary cause of John's negative behaviour is the breakdown of the relationship between John and his teachers.

Dwyfor-Davies, J. and Lee, J. (2006) To attend or not to attend? Why some students choose school and others reject it. *Support for Learning*, 21 (4).
  In this study, Dwyfor-Davies and Lee examine the perspectives of 13 non-attending students and their parents, 35 students who have a satisfactory attendance record, and a range of educational professionals.

Action Point

Return to your 'critical incident' diary. You now need to begin to analyse the incidents that you have recorded, using the literature to scaffold your thinking. Useful questions to ask might be as follows.

- Why is it easy to 'blame' the learner, or their family, for incidents of general disenchantment with the education process?
- How might a young person be marginalised by the education system? What can be done to reduce this?
- What assumptions do you hold about each incident? Why?

Key strategies for developing this content area

As has been mentioned in earlier chapters, getting a starting point for assignments can be very challenging. However, many students have commented that a 'critical incident' diary offers a useful scaffold for examining difficult issues such as inclusion and behaviour, and can help you develop better insights, and as such, inform your practice.

This diary can be a place where you capture incidents that on first thoughts may, or indeed may not, be critical in terms of informing your thinking or practice. Later reflections and considerations of these incidents should help you to identify what their significance is, and what their meaning and implication might be. Your diary should therefore contain some brief background information, a description of the incident, and your increasingly deep reflections on it.

The critical incident diary can then be used as the basis of a critical incident analysis approach to compiling a portfolio or assignment to support your work in this content area. Let us return to how we understand the term 'critical incident'. It is important that we have some way of recognising what makes an incident 'critical'. I have previously suggested that critical incident is one that challenges your own assumptions or makes you think differently. One framework or structure for using critical incident analysis is outlined below. You will find more details of this in Chapter 2.

- What happened and where and when? Give a brief history of the incident.
- What is it that has made the incident 'critical'?
- What were your immediate thoughts and responses?
- What are your thoughts now? What has changed/developed your thinking?
- What have you learned about (your) practice from this?
- How might your practice change and develop as a result of this analysis and learning?

Stop and Read

Moon, J. (2004) *A Handbook of Reflective and Experiential Learning: Theory and practice.* Abingdon: RoutledgeFalmer.

This text is full of excellent examples, and in particular, it helps you move your reflective writing beyond the descriptive to the more critically reflective – see Resource 9 at the end.

Moon, J. (2008) *Critical thinking: An exploration of theory and practice.* Abingdon: Routledge.

A useful and accessible read in helping to develop your own critical thinking skills.

Poulson L. and Wallace M. (2004) *Learning to Read Critically in Teaching and Learning.* London: Sage.

This is a very useful guide to critical reading and its relationship to and support for critical writing.

Assignments

Suggested assignments to address this content area

When you undertake your MTL, you will be encouraged to engage in school-based practice development work which can be the basis for assignments/assessment opportunities for MTL modules. The following list may provide some useful prompts.

- A case study of a child in your class, focusing, in particular, on relationships in the classroom.
- An analysis of the barriers to inclusion for child X.

- An analysis of child X's views on inclusion.
- An evaluation of the impact of an ecosystemic approach on your practice.
- An evaluation of the impact of the SEAL (Social and Emotional Aspects of Learning) Programme.

Summary

At the end of this chapter, you now have developed an:
- awareness of the complexity of child development;
- understanding of self-concept, relationships and teacher–student attachment;
- understanding of the literature, research and legislation surrounding the inclusion of students described as having behavioural difficulties;
- awareness of the values, attitudes, principles and practicalities of inclusion for individuals designated as having BESD;

Further reading

Armstrong, F. and Moore, M. (2004) *Action Research for Inclusive Education: Changing places, changing practice, changing minds*. Abingdon: RoutledgeFalmer.

Steer, A. (2009) *Review of Pupil Behaviour (interim report 4)*. London: Institute of Education.

Stubbs, S. and Lewis, I. (eds) (2009) *Inclusive Education: Where there are few resources*. London: Enabling Education Network.

Useful websites

Alliance for Inclusive Education: **www.afasic.org.uk**
Behaviour for Learning: **www.behaviour4learning.ac.uk**
Centre for Studies on Inclusive Education: **www.csie.org.uk**
Equality and Human Rights Commission: **www.equalityhumanrights.com**

CHAPTER 6

Content area 4: Leadership, management and working with others

School leadership is beyond the undertakings of one heroic individual. It is simply not possible, and may not even be desirable, for one individual to undertake every leadership task within a school. Good school leaders are those who are able to maximise the diverse leadership qualities of others, enabling them to take on leadership within their own areas of expertise. They lead by managing, motivating and inspiring people. This may come through individual one-to-one work with teachers, pupils, parents, governors, or through creating the impetus within an organisation that encourages and enables people to play an active part in school life.

(Riley and MacBeath, in MacBeath (ed.), 1998, p148)

...if you want to be a leader, you have to be a real human being. You must recognize the true meaning of life before you can become a great leader. You must understand yourself first.

(Senge *et al.*, 2004, p186)

Chapter Objectives

By the end of this chapter, you should have:
- **begun to understand how your own leadership capacity might be developed;**
- **an awareness of a range of leadership concepts, and an understanding of their applicability in your own context;**
- **an understanding of some of the tools available to facilitate self-assessment in relation to teamwork and leadership;**
- **developed a greater understanding of integrated and multi-agency and team working and be able to identify your own and the school's role within this context;**
- **a greater understanding of the professionals and services available to children and young people and be able to identify ways to identify structures and individual contacts (within and outside your school) to support children with additional needs;**
- **a greater awareness of the skills and knowledge required to work in an integrated way with other practitioners and be able to identify personal learning needs in this area.**

Links to the professional standards
The key standards addressed in this content area are listed below.

Professional attributes
C5, C6

Professional knowledge and understanding
C20, C21, C22, C23, C24, C25

Professional skills
C37, C40, C41

Introduction

This strand of your MTL moves you beyond the classroom, and encourages you to explore your practice in collaboration with others, and to explore and develop your leadership capacity. It draws on the fact that you have now begun to learn more about yourself as a teacher, and are starting to develop effective working relationships with other professionals, and have perhaps also started to take on some additional responsibilities and duties. While it is likely that your formal leadership or management experience may be limited in the early years of your career, it is almost certain that you will have some opportunities to lead some work with colleagues in relation to curriculum or other issues.

The chapter is constructed in two sections. Section 1 focuses on the role of leadership and management within schools, exploring leadership and management styles, approaches, models and concepts and how leadership at different levels of the school system impacts on teaching and learning. It presents a fairly concise overview of some theoretical perspectives (a more complete review would be impossible in a text like this), and highlights specifically the concept of emerging and developing leadership.

Section 2 explores working with others: the role of the teacher in collaboration with other practitioners (something that will be a significant aspect of your practice), groups and agencies, particularly in the light of Every Child Matters, the vision for the twenty-first century school and recent reforms to the children's workforce.

Section 1: The role of leadership and management in schools

This section is intended to provide you with some:

- theoretical perspectives and understandings around the concepts and models of leadership and management;

- prompts and opportunities to explore how you might develop your own emerging leadership and management capacity.

You may already have some leadership skills and attributes. Indeed, given that you have qualified as a teacher, it would be surprising if you did not have. Some of the activities in this chapter will help you to articulate more fully these skills and attributes, and support you in finding ways in which you can develop them more fully in an educational context. As the quotation above from Riley and MacBeath (1998) suggests, school leadership is about much more than the vision or actions of the head teacher. High quality teaching requires excellent management skills (including planning, time- and self-management, behaviour management and resources management) at all levels in the school or organisation, and it also demands the teacher to lead pupils and other colleagues through their vision and actions in support of learning, both within their classroom and across the school in general.

'Leadership' and 'management' are terms that are sometimes used interchangeably. Most theorists however, see a distinction, although they also see them as linked concepts. Everard *et al.* (2004) argue that leadership is an indispensable aspect of management.

The concept of leadership is distinct from that of management, which tends to be viewed as a more instrumental process of establishing and maintaining systems and structures. Leadership is typified by vision, purpose and influence whereas management is on day-to-day operations, processes and administration. West-Burnham (1977) (highlighting that this debate is not a new one), makes the distinction below.

Leading is concerned with:	Managing is concerned with:
vision	implementation
	systems
ends	means
people doing the right things	doing things right
strategic issues	operational issues
transformation	transaction

Following what Hopkins *et al.* (2009, p2) describe as *a somewhat laissez faire and paternalistic culture of leadership* in the 1980s, the mid-1990s witnessed the emergence of 'educational leadership', or 'school leadership', as a key concept in educational policy. This was in part due to the implementation of neo-liberal models of education with additional autonomy and decentralisation combined with increased accountability and performance management frameworks. This model of schooling demands different roles and responsibilities for school leaders, who arguably have greater autonomy to make school-based decisions, yet are expected to comply with (and excel at) a range of performance management and reporting requirements. The school leader needed, therefore, to lead a vision for the school, inspire and motivate those in and around the school and be able to respond to the increasing demands of managerialism from central government.

The increased emphasis on leadership (as distinct to management) was highlighted with the emergence of the National College for School Leadership (NCSL) in 2000, with its focus on supporting and developing existing and emerging leaders within the sector. Much of this development and professionalisation of the school leader has focused on the roles of the head teacher, assistant or deputy heads or other senior management team (SMT) members. In part due to the increasing complexity of school leadership (Bush and Middlewood, 2005), there has also been a drive towards other, distributed models of leadership, with teachers and other staff adopting roles as subject or curriculum team leaders, or having responsibility for specific areas of activity or development across the school. Often tasked with the challenging role of 'leading from the middle' these 'learning leadership' roles can present the challenge of responsibility without authority, whereby the member of staff is expected to lead or make changes to an area of teaching and learning practice without having any management responsibility. Such roles are often the first steps towards management within the school and demand considerable leadership skills and ability. It is in such roles that many of you may have opportunities to hone your leadership capacity during the early years of your career.

We will start by focusing on leadership, looking at some models and theoretical perspectives, and illustrating this with some case studies or examples. High-quality leadership is regularly identified as a key aspect of effective or successful schools (e.g. Bush and Glover, 2004). Aside from questions about what makes a school effective, what does 'high quality' leadership look like?

As Northouse (2009) identifies, the term 'leadership' has many different meanings and, as such, is difficult to define. While definitions of leadership (or educational leadership) focus on different areas, such as personality traits, power relationships, strategy and vision or objectives, they often contain similar or overlapping dimensions:

Leadership is a process whereby an individual influences a group of individuals to achieve a common goal.

(Northouse, 2009, p3)

By leadership, I mean influencing others' actions in achieving desirable ends. Leaders are people who shape the goals, motivations and actions of others. Frequently they initiate change to reach existing and new goals.

(Cuban, 1988)

[Leadership is] a process of influence leading to the achievement of desired purposes. Successful leaders develop a vision for their schools based upon personal and professional values. They articulate this vision at every opportunity and influence their staff and other stakeholders to share the vision. The philosophy, structures and activities of the school are geared towards the achievement of this shared vision.

(Bush and Glover, 2003, p8)

In 2009, Northouse identified five different ways of responding to the question 'What is a leader?' suggesting that leadership may be seen as:

* traits;
* abilities;
* skills;
* behaviours;
* relationships.

He briefly discusses the difference in these ways of defining leadership, and then asks his readers to use these frameworks to explore their own understanding of what leadership is. Exercises like this are helpful in clarifying your own perspective, and in developing not just your abstract understanding, but also in making more concrete links to your practice.

A helpful concept to understand as you begin to take more of a leadership role is that of 'distributed leadership'. Although this is not a new idea as such, it has become a much more widely recognised approach to leadership in schools and other settings. The NCSL web-based materials cite three ideas which are central in the philosophy of distributed leadership.

1. *The belief in leadership teams: belief in the power of one is giving way to a belief in the power of everyone.*
2. *As schools become more complex places to manage and lead, we need many more leaders than ever before.*
3. *Ensuring that there are many leaders enables us to create pools of talent, from which we can grow tomorrow's leaders.*
      (**http://forms.ncsl.org.uk/mediastore/image2/distributedleadership_web/ animation.htm**)

Each of these ideas should have some resonance with you when you reflect on schools you work or have worked in. Southwark (in Davies, 2009) suggests that not only does distributed leadership allow for the sharing of a key function, and also the development of future senior leaders, but that also it provides a means for the distribution of a particular type of leadership, 'learning-centred leadership'. This, he claims, is the key means by which schools can make a positive difference in classrooms.

It is about increasing the density of leadership so that everyone has access to facilitative leaders who can help them articulate and analyse their professional experience, and act on it to improve the quality of teaching and learning.
                                                        (Southwark, in Davies, 2009, p108)

While early in your career, it is clear that your main work focus is 'the quality of teaching and learning', you must also remember that since teaching and learning are the core business of schools, then this is central to the whole leadership and management function also. Your early forays into leadership may be based upon your own classroom practice, and perhaps supporting the sharing of practice with colleagues. This type of activity will help you hone your leadership skills, and also begin to realise what a difference all teachers can make to the quality of teaching and learning in schools.

Case Study

Laura the leader

In Chapter 4, we looked at how a newly qualified teacher, Laura, developed her subject knowledge through accessing her subject association and working with colleagues in other schools. In the reflection on Laura's study, you may recall the following statement.

> A further, and interesting outcome of this was the impact it had on Laura's career pathway. The deputy head of the school was the RE co-ordinator, and asked Laura to also work closely with her in a shadowing/advisory capacity, given her developing subject expertise in RE. Within a few years she was appointed coordinator for PE in recognition of her leadership skills.

Let us now find out some more about this move into formal leadership from Laura's perspective. Having taken the initiative in organising meetings with colleagues from outside her own school, and begin to develop not only her subject knowledge but an appreciation of how this type of development could be further enhanced by collaborative reflection and evaluation, she began to realise how she might take a leading role in organising this.

> We started by simply sharing thoughts and resources, but I had an idea that we could take this further, and rather than just meet and share information, we could be more developmental, and from our meetings, develop new schemes, which we could implement and evaluate. I suggested it to the others, and they agreed. I asked my head if our school could do this, and said I would organise getting all the necessary data.

Reflection

Consider Northouse's (2009) response to the question 'What is a leader?', and suggest how you think Laura demonstrated leadership through her actions. It is interesting that her thoughts around the sharing of practice made her consider how this could be improved and developed. Many situations we find ourselves in offer opportunities to go beyond the basic expectation, and in thinking about such opportunities, it is possible to see the potential for leadership development. It is also interesting to see that Laura's move into leadership was not planned, but arose because of the way in which she dealt with a situation in her practice. How might someone plan to develop their leadership capacity?

Stop and Read

An Introduction to Leadership Concepts and Practices, by Peter Northouse (2009) is an
accessible text which includes a range of practical activities you can undertake in
order to both explore and develop your own understanding of leadership.

Action Point

You should ask your head of department or key stage if you might shadow them in some of
their leadership work, and ask if they would be willing to discuss the experience with you
after.

- Reflect on the range of tasks that they undertook.
- Reflect on the skills and attributes you think they needed in carrying out these tasks.
- Reflect on the interpersonal nature of their work.

Planning leadership development

There are many texts presenting a range of models of leadership, some of which focus more
on issues of management than leadership, others which focus on ethical leadership, models
such as 'transformational' and 'transactional' and models which look at traits, attributes and
abilities. All are useful, but as Bush (2008) suggests, each is partial, providing what
Sergiovanni (1984, p6) describes as *a limited view, dwelling excessively on some aspects of
leadership to the virtual exclusion of others*. Rather than seeing this as problematic *per se*,
Bush suggests that it provides a useful starting point for leadership development, particularly
focusing on leadership to improve the quality of learning. In order to do this, he suggests
linking the instructional model of leadership (which relates to the direction, rather than the
process of leadership) to the transformational model of leadership (which addresses the
process, as well as the direction of leadership).

It may be that in reading around such theoretical perspectives, you, as an early-career
teacher, feel that your main focus at this stage in your career is the development of effective
teaching and learning strategies. However, you will no doubt be aware of the importance of
effective leadership in making sure that learning and teaching have the desired impact on
pupils. Leithwood *et al.* (2006. p4) suggest that *school leadership is second only to classroom
teaching as an influence on pupil learning* and further add that:

> There is not a single documented case of a school successfully turning round its pupil
> achievement trajectory in the absence of talented leadership.
>
> (Leithwood *et al.*, 2006, p5)

You will see therefore that the quality of school leadership is a key factor in promoting pupil achievement, and is therefore something that should concern all teachers. Further, it can be seen that the concept of planned leadership development is crucial if schools are to have effective leadership both at present and in the future. The range of leadership development opportunities offered by local authorities, and the NCSL among others, addresses this agenda for teachers at varying stages in their careers. It is important therefore to do as Laura did, and explore your emerging leadership capacity through the various situations and opportunities that present themselves. When you reflect on the earlier points raised by Northouse (2009), traits, abilities, skills, behaviours and relationships – you might like to think of ways in which you can first of all assess, and then develop these aspects of your practice. The action point below suggests one way in which you might do this. However, your MTL colleagues, mentor or university tutor may also have other suggestions about how you might assess your capacity, and support you in actively planning to develop it. There are many self-assessment tools available freely in texts and online which you may like to explore. In particular, you may wish to explore some of the psychometric tools such as Myers–Briggs Type Indicators, or the Keirsey Temperament Test (**www.humanmetrics.com/cgi-win/ JTypes2.asp**). A further useful tool to explore is the Belbin Team Roles Inventory (visit **www.belbin.com/** for further information), which is a useful way to begin to understand your own strengths and weaknesses in team working.

Stop and Read

You should now have a brief overview of leadership development. The following books and sources will help you improve your knowledge and understanding in relation to this.

Brundrett, M., Burton, N. and Smith, R. (eds) (2003) *Leadership in Education*. London: Sage.
　This text provides a structured overview of leadership concepts, and perspectives on leadership perspectives in four sections.
　1. Conceptualising leadership.
　2. Developing leadership, developing leaders.
　3. Teachers as leaders.
　4. Perspectives on leadership in practice.

Each of the four sections explores key issues, through three separately authored chapters, which will allow you to read it in a way that best suits your needs and interests.

Robertson, J. (2008) *Coaching Educational Leadership: Building leadership capacity through partnership*. London: Sage.
　This book introduces you to the theoretical perspectives on coaching, the concepts of educational leadership and leadership learning, before moving into a second section which provides a rich set of practical activities which help relate theory and practice.

Action Point

Ask someone in your school who is in a clear leadership role if you can observe their practice over a period of time, perhaps while they undertake a particular task. In conjunction with them, use one of the frameworks from Northouse's book to analyse their leadership style. Discuss with them the analysis, and suggest areas where they were strong, and areas which could be developed. Identify the key leadership learning points for you, in having completed this exercise.

Power and power relationships

It would be incomplete to discuss leadership and management without a brief mention of power and power relationships. *Power is the capacity to influence or affect others* (Northouse, 2009, p166). Drawing on the work of French and Raven (1959), he cites five bases of power.

1. Referent power, which is based on followers' identification and liking for a leader.
2. Expert power, which is based on the followers' perceptions of the leader's competence.
3. Legitimate power, which is associated with having status or formal job authority.
4. Reward power, which derives from having the capacity to provide benefits to others.
5. Coercive power, which derives from being able to penalise or punish others.

An important part of moving into a leadership role is the extent to which teachers assume a greater degree of power than they may previously have had. Alongside this power comes responsibility. As you move into a position of more formal leadership, you will be expected to take on additional responsibilities, and these may include having management responsibility for curriculum or administrative matters, or for managing other members of staff. It is this third category of responsibility that brings with it the professional responsibility of effectively managing the relationships between yourself and your various colleagues, in a way that makes a positive contribution to school life. It is perhaps an appropriate place in which to mention the concept of 'middle leadership' as a central one in terms of interdependent and changing relationships.

Middle leadership

As schools have become more complex organisations, and concepts of leadership and management have grown to include the notions of distributed leadership and middle leadership, it has become commonplace for the tier of leaders, known as middle leaders, to have key roles to play in schools, and as such, to be offered opportunities for training and development. As both teacher and leader, they play a vital role in both the strategic and operational levels of school management, in many cases acting almost as a mediatory layer. Blandford (2006), citing Chatwin (2004), discusses the extent to which middle leaders act in networked relationships throughout the school, and exert influence beyond their immediate teams through a series of interdependencies.

- *Their positioning within the communication networks which give access to information and the possibility of conveying (and interpreting) it to others.*
- *Their degree of mastery of the techniques and approaches needed to exert upward influence.*
- *The extent to which they are seen as competent by top management.*
- *The degree of open or closed mindedness of senior management.*
- *The extent to which they are trusted by senior management, this trust being related to time in post.*

(Blandford, 2006, pp6–7)

In reflecting on these five key points, you should begin to realise that taking on a middle leadership role requires you to be confident and competent in your teaching and classroom practice, trusted by colleagues, peers and senior management, a good communicator, and someone who relates well to people at all levels of the organisation. There will inevitably be tensions in such a role as you struggle to assimilate the much wider range of perspectives needed. Blandford (2006) lists a range of additional responsibilities that middle leaders take on, including:

- staff support and management;
- curriculum development;
- curriculum management;
- resources;
- pupil progress;
- record keeping;
- liaison;
- safety.

You will see from that that you must keep your feet firmly in your classroom practice, and yet must also take an active, and at times proactive role in decision-making, policy formulation, and in issues such as the mentoring and managing of less experienced staff. It is likely that your role will entail you having some curriculum responsibility, and as such, it can reinforce and be reinforced by the good practice of keeping yourself updated on curriculum, pedagogic and other classroom-related issues.

Reflection

If you do not already have some curriculum leadership responsibility, plan to interview someone in your school who does have. What questions might you want to ask them? What factual information might you want? What do they see as the high points of their role? Are there any difficulties/problems that they encounter? How might your insights help you prepare for a leadership role?

Section 2: Working with others

Multi-agency working is about different services, agencies and teams of professionals and other staff working together to provide the services that fully meet the needs of children, young people and their parents or carers.

To work successfully on a multi-agency basis you need to be clear about your own role and aware of the roles of other professionals, you need to be confident about your own standards and targets and respectful of those that apply to other services, actively seeking and respecting the knowledge and input others can make to delivering best outcomes for children and young people.

(Common Core of Skills and Knowledge for the Children's Workforce, DfES, 2005, p18)

This section examines the changing context of the school and the children's workforce and explores the role of you as a teacher within this. It also explores the different aspects of collaborative practice, from work with other colleagues in the classroom, to multi-agency working and partnerships with parents.

The section also briefly explores the role of the teacher in safeguarding the well-being of children and young people, as well as discussing the role of the school and teacher in 'early intervention' and the prevention of negative outcomes for children. The Common Assessment Framework (CAF) and the role of the lead professional are also discussed.

The section is also intended to link to the skills and knowledge requirements within the *Common Core of Skills and Knowledge for the Children's Workforce* (DfES, 2005a).

Introduction

The role of the teacher is often seen as a solo effort, with the teacher working independently in the classroom. However, effective collaboration with a range of other colleagues is often the key to the delivery of high-quality teaching and learning opportunities for pupils. This collaboration may take place:

- within the classroom with teaching assistants or other support staff;
- with other teaching colleagues in relation to curriculum planning, subject leadership or pupil liaison;
- with other school support staff responsible for specific aspects of school life (e.g. bursar, administrators, etc.);
- with other professions working in or around the school to provide services and support for pupils, parents and staff in a range of specialist areas.

With the emergence of Every Child Matters, Extended Schools and the recent introduction of the vision for the Twenty-first century School (see below), the school is undergoing significant changes. These changes are likely to increase the amount of collaboration between teachers, teaching assistants and other professional groups, both within the school and in the wider community. Partnership between the school and parents is also likely to become a greater priority as these policies develop.

Effective collaboration with others, in the classroom, school and beyond, provides excellent opportunities to support the development of a model of inclusive education which provides:

> *a framework within which all children – regardless of ability, gender, language, ethnic or cultural origin – can be valued equally, treated with respect and provided with real opportunities at school.*
>
> (Thomas and Loxley, 2001, p119)

As Todd (2007) suggests, effective collaborative or partnership working is not always straightforward or effective in the ways it supports this goal. There can often be different perspectives, priorities and targets at play, some of which might conflict with the goals of inclusive education. Effective collaboration and partnership therefore require an awareness of others' roles, excellent communication and negotiation skills, trust and a shared purpose in relation to outcomes for children and young people. Throughout this section, the key issues in effective collaborative practice are explored, and actions and activities identified which support partnership working in and around the classroom and the school.

The changing context

The past ten years have seen a range of changes to schools and those who work within them. In 2003, for example, schools saw the implementation of 'workforce remodelling', with changes to the terms and conditions for teachers in maintained schools in support of a focus on leading and managing the learning process. This remodelling process was intended to tackle the excessive workload of teachers and ensure that they were able to focus on their main teaching role. This included providing identified time for planning, preparation and assessment as well as a contractual right to 'leadership and management' time, and national guidance on areas such as administration and cover. Perhaps most significantly for classroom practice, workforce remodelling recognised that other staff who were not qualified as teachers could support classroom learning and also teach, led by the teacher in their role as the leader (or manager) of classroom learning. The role of the teaching assistant was therefore enhanced, and a new qualification, the Higher Level Teaching Assistant (HLTA), was introduced to provide specialist assistance to support teachers and other school activities.

At the same time, the report by Lord Laming into the death of Victoria Climbié triggered the publication of the *Every Child Matters* Green Paper (DfES, 2003), and with it the start of the ECM agenda and the raft of accompanying initiatives. Every Child Matters advocates a joined-up (or integrated) approach to responding to the needs of young people, bringing services and organisations together to respond to five outcomes:

- be healthy;
- stay safe;
- enjoy and achieve;
- make a positive contribution;
- achieve economic and social well-being.

The document *Every Child Matters: Change for Children in Schools* (DfES, 2004b) recognises the connection between a child's well-being and their performance (and attainment) as a pupil in school. The school is therefore recognised not only as a place of teaching and learning but where the well-being of the child is of equal importance and its consideration is a key part in ensuring that children are able to achieve positive outcomes. This point was further reinforced within the Education and Inspection Act 2006, introducing a duty on schools to promote the well-being of children and young people.

Every Child Matters, together with other reform in areas such as health, has meant significant and ongoing changes at both an organisational level across children's services and for members of the children's workforce. The Children Act 2004 saw the introduction of Children's Trusts bringing together in partnership a wide range of services working with young people (including education, social services, health, youth offending teams and many others) through a 'duty to co-operate' to contribute to children's and young people's outcomes (extended to schools through the Apprenticeships, Skills, Children and Learning Act 2009). The intention is to promote an approach where strategy, planning, commissioning and delivery of services to children and young people are integrated, with all partners working together appropriately. This agenda is focused within a framework that supports high-quality provision for all, on the prevention of issues and concerns to (and caused by) children and young people, and the early intervention into, and prevention of such problems or concerns. For local authorities, and those with a duty to co-operate, the changes have meant the development of an overarching children's services body, led by a director (DCS) to oversee all services to children and young people.

It has also meant the introduction of a range of new initiatives to promote integrated working, collaboration and communication across all services working with children and young people. These initiatives include the development of children's centres, a Common Assessment Framework (CAF), and the continued development of Extended Schools. We shall examine some of these later in the chapter.

For many working within the children's workforce, the change has been considerable. Some roles and services have been redefined and other new professional roles are emerging. The roles and responsibilities of, for example, school nurses, health visitors, youth workers, education welfare officers and others have changed significantly over the past ten years. The Early Years Professional (EYP) was established to improve the professional pathways for those working with children aged 0–5 and to improve the quality of Early Years provision. The role of a lead professional, which can be undertaken by any professional, has also emerged to work with services, children and young people to obtain appropriate responses to meet their needs.

Every Child Matters and the Twenty-first century School

For many schools, perhaps the most noticeable changes have so far come about as part of the Extended Schools programme, intended to meet the ECM outcomes through a school-based (or at least school-linked) offer, including:

* a varied range of out-of-school activities;
* for primary schools, availability of 'wraparound' care provision between 8 a.m. and 6 p.m. (for example, breakfast and after-school clubs);
* parenting support;
* access to targeted support for children (e.g. speech and language therapists);
* community access to facilities.

The Children's Plan (DCSF, 2007a) suggests, however, that this is just the beginning of the school's role, placing schools at the heart of future initiatives. It introduced the notion of the Twenty-first century School which was further developed in the White Paper *Your Child, Your Schools, Our Future: Building a 21st Century Schools System* (2009).

The Twenty-first century School (from DCSF, 2007a)

Schools play a central role in helping children achieve their potential and enjoy their childhood. A school's distinctive contribution is in excellent teaching and learning, ensuring children achieve. But schools are also places where children develop confidence, self-respect and respect for others, learn about teamwork and leadership, and about responsibility and successful relationships.

Schools are a vital community resource. Almost all children and young people spend time in school, both during the school day and outside it. Most families trust and are familiar with their school, and schools are also accessible to the wider community. Schools can therefore offer wider opportunities for children, young people and their families to take part in sport or cultural activities as well as learning. Because schools know their pupils well, and understand what opportunities they need and what may prevent them from succeeding, they are places where emerging problems can be identified and addressed early and swiftly, either by the school itself or by engaging specialist help.

The 21st century school is a school that excels in each of these dimensions. It provides an excellent education and by personalising learning does not compromise in its mission to see each child achieve all of which he or she is capable. But it also actively contributes to all aspects of a child's life – health and wellbeing, safety, and developing the wider experiences and skills that characterise a good childhood and set a young person up for success as an adult. It contributes to these wider areas because they help children achieve, but also because they are good for children's wider development and part of a good childhood.

The school actively engages and listens to parents, makes sure their views shape school policies, and works with them as partners in their child's learning and development. It looks beyond the pupils on its roll, and works in partnership with other schools to ensure education in the local area is as good as it can be. It plays a central role in the wider community, opening its facilities for the benefit of families and others, and is conscious of its role in a sustainable society.

Every child should have a personal tutor, someone in the school who knows them well, helps them to identify and plan to meet their ambitions and to act quickly if problems emerge, talking to parents and bringing in other support where necessary.

The 21st century school can only fulfil its potential if it can rely on other, often specialist, services for children being there when needed – including health (for example mental health and speech and language therapy), early years and childcare, behaviour, youth, and crime prevention services. It needs to be an active partner in planning and delivery arrangements under Children's Trusts, helping to define the priorities for their local area, and agreeing how the whole pattern of local services best fits together to meet need. If we are to achieve our 2020 goals for children and young people, every school will need to realise this vision of a 21st century school.

The Twenty-first century School is underpinned by:

- a personalised learning approach with a wide variety of learning opportunities;
- a focus on the personal and social development of children and young people;
- a high level of parent and carer engagement partnership with other education and childcare providers, as well as with children's services;
- the provision of a range of activities for children, young people and the wider community;
- early identification of additional needs and the meeting of these needs either directly or with a network of partners.

Implications for the teacher

With the very significant exception of the further development of personalised learning, much of the vision for the Twenty-first century School implies activity outside the classroom. This does not mean, however, that school teachers should not be aware of, and engaged with, this change agenda. If the vision is realised, the overall context in which teaching takes place is likely to change significantly. Schools may, for example, need to be as focused on supporting children's well-being as they have been on pupil attainment. Furthermore, the notion of 'school' itself may come to mean more than solely a place where teaching takes place, with a wide range of services and activities being provided for children, parents and members of the community. Indeed, some authorities have already sought to abolish the term 'school' in order to try to reshape people's thinking and expectations about what takes place in these settings.

It is hoped that such an approach will provide many benefits for both children and teachers. Schools will have closer links with other support staff and services, some of whom may be co-located within the school itself. This closer working should enable better responses to the well-being needs of children and, in turn, contribute to their participation and attainment within the classroom. As Todd (2007) identifies, however, there can also be potentially conflicting priorities within partnership working. Some agencies may, for example, see child protection, crime prevention, health surveillance or employment outcomes as the priority. Indeed, with a focus on schools as a site of 'prevention' and 'early intervention' in avoiding 'negative outcomes' such as teenage pregnancy, crime and anti-social behaviour, childhood obesity and youth unemployment, it is easy to see how schools' main purpose of education could become diverted (or at least distracted). (For a further critical analysis of prevention and early intervention see Parton, 2006.)

It is unlikely that the core role of the teacher will change as a result of much of this development – supporting the educational needs of individual children and classes will remain the primary focus. Indeed, children's workforce reform to date has strongly emphasised that changes are about enhancing professional roles through closer working, not doing away with professional specialism. It is likely, however, that there will be an expectation for teachers to be more aware of the roles of other professionals in, around and outside the school and to be able to promote the well-being of children and young people in their teaching and in their wider role within the school.

For many teachers, particularly those with special educational needs roles (e.g. SENCOs or those in special schools), much of this will already be taking place. They will also be aware of the fast-changing environment and that there is still a great deal to do in order to ensure that integrated working is effective in meeting the needs of children and young people.

The rest of this chapter examines different dimensions of the changes mentioned above and the implications for teachers in relation to working with others:

* in and around the classroom;
* in the broader school context;
* with others beyond the school setting.

Reflection

* Consider your own school in relation to the notion of the Twenty-first century School. What steps is the school taking towards the government's vision?
* What are the implications for your role as a teacher? How might this vision change, support or perhaps hinder your teaching role?
* To what extent do you think 'good teaching' in the classroom is linked to (or can be separated from) the broader pastoral/well-being dimension of children and young people?

- What steps have you taken towards understanding and engaging with 'personalised learning'? What more do you need to do?
- Are there any possible problems with this vision for a Twenty-first century School? What might they be?

Stop and Read

Todd, L. (2007) *Partnerships for Inclusive Education: A critical approach to collaborative working.* Abingdon: Routledge.

Liz Todd provides an interesting and analytical exploration of partnership, collaborative and integrated working, raising questions about whether it leads to inclusion. The book links theory and practice effectively, with some up-to-date examples of practice.

Collaboration and leadership in and around the classroom

Changes brought about prior to and as a consequence of workforce remodelling (see above) and other measures related to children's workforce reform have seen the number of school support staff nearly double since 1997. Described in various ways and through various functions (such as learning support assistant, general assistant, cover supervisor or classroom helper), classroom support usually takes the form of whole-class, small group or individually focused support. In some areas, such as Early Years, additional roles such as nursery nurses and the Early Years Professional (EYP) may also be present.

Most significantly, the growth of support staff has seen an increase in the role of teaching assistants (TAs) across both primary and secondary school (though they are still most strongly focused on primary). The total number of teaching assistants has risen from 122,400 within maintained nursery, primary, middle and secondary schools, special schools and pupil referral units in January 2003 to 177,000 in the state-funded sector in 2008.

From being regarded as 'domestic helpers', usually for those with physical or sensory impairment (Brennan, 1982), the role has developed into that of 'assistant teacher', able to contribute to the planning and delivery of whole-class, small group and individual teaching under the overall leadership and responsibility of a qualified teacher. The transition has also been reflected in TA training and the recently introduced Higher Level Teaching Assistant qualification (HLTA), which seeks to recognise the specialist skills of teaching assistants, enable them to take on more responsibilities and also provide a further career pathway for this work.

Of course, not all teaching assistants will perform the role of the assistant teacher for the whole class. Some TAs will be specifically employed to support individuals with special educational needs, and the teacher will need to collaborate with them in relation to developing a planned learning approach for the individual child. The teacher will also need to ensure that the TA/pupil relationship is managed in a manner that avoids over-dependency, a high level of attachment and the child becoming identified as different in a manner that prevents inclusive practice.

Some non-teaching teaching assistants (and other support staff) may focus their activity primarily on preparation for learning. This may, for example, involve preparing materials for those with special needs, helping children to prepare for activities such as PE or other such support.

Another emerging support role is that of the learning mentor. Learning mentors may operate within the classroom to support individuals or, more frequently, outside the class-room environment, though still with a learning-focused role. Learning mentors tend to support pupils who are at risk of poor attainment, underachievement or who face personal barriers to achievement. The role is intended to complement other school systems and staff and usually provides one-to-one support for individuals. This can be through the provision of advice and guidance, learning support around school or homework and through the agreement of action plans in areas such as attendance and participation. Their role can also include responsibilities for classroom support and the transfer of information and assessment (Hughes, 2005).

This emerging complexity provides new challenges and opportunities for teachers in support of personalised learning for children and young people. The provision of additional classroom support, either for individuals or the whole class, does not necessarily improve student learning or free teachers up to spend more focused time with students. Indeed, if not well co-ordinated it can mean that teachers end up dedicating more time to support staff than to pupil learning, which:

> can perhaps be explained by the complex set of interpersonal and professional uncer-tainties which are introduced when extra people work alongside the classroom teacher.
>
> (Vincett *et al.*, 2005, p5)

High-quality collaboration between the teacher and support staff is therefore vital in order to ensure that resources are used in an effective way to support pupil learning. This requires a range of skills and abilities on the part of the teacher.

- Recognition of the needs of individuals and the class as a whole.
- Awareness of the roles of those working in and around the classroom.
- Understanding of the particular skills and abilities (and limitations) of support staff.
- Awareness of their own skills, abilities and limitations.
- Awareness of relationships between staff and particular children in order to get the best out of a child's learning and behaviour.
- The ability to communicate their overall purpose and intentions about teaching and learning approaches, classroom and behaviour management.
- The ability to prioritise and to delegate work in a clear and effective manner.
- The ability to support staff sensitively and contribute to their professional development.

- When working with children with special educational needs, ensure that all staff have sufficient understanding, skills and support to work in the specific context.
- Commitment to a team approach that values the different contributions of all members.
- The ability to ensure that the child's learning and development are placed at the heart of the team's approach.

The formulation of an effective team rarely takes place without space and time to explore these areas, both individually and as a group. Consider the following.

- Allowing opportunities to discuss purpose, roles and other elements of team operation.
- Spending time together in training.
- Involving support staff in planning so that methods and approaches are clearly understood.
- Spending time each morning discussing the day's work with the team, being clear about the purpose of activities and expectations of team members.
- Involving support staff in reviews of work, providing constructive feedback to aid individual and team development.
- Celebrating successes together.

Vincett *et al.* (2005) identify and evaluate three models of collaborative classroom practice involving support staff (particularly teaching assistants).

1. Room management, where specific roles are adopted for activities, with one or more 'learning managers' concentrating on intensive work with individual students (or small groups) for specified periods of time, and 'activity manager(s)' overseeing the task and supporting those not receiving intensive support from the learning manager.
2. Zoning, adopting a geographical model of classroom organisation, where different zones are identified, with staff given responsibility for a zone (or zones) depending upon the activity and learning needs of individuals and groups. Students are then grouped depending upon the intended outcomes of the activities.
3. Reflective teamwork, concentrating on improving classroom delivery through improved communication, planning and review. Teachers and TAs spend time developing trust and a greater understanding of how each other operates, regularly coming together to plan and review teaching and learning. This is underpinned by a commitment to co-operation and to reflective practice that allows open and honest exploration of each other's practice. This model also reflects many of the attributes of good collaborative working across the children's workforce.

While it is apparent that there is no single effective way of maximising the effectiveness of team practice within the classroom, it is clear that teachers can improve learning and teaching through the considered development of collaboration with classroom colleagues.

As is the case with collaborative practice in general, this is often underpinned by trust, open and honest communication and reflective practice between staff.

Case Study

Yvonne has a problem

Yvonne is a newly appointed English teacher in a large secondary school. Sophie, a member of her Year 7 tutor group, has come to the attention of a number of staff because of her disengaged and sometimes problematic behaviour in class. She appears tired and reluctant to respond to questions and on occasions has reacted with verbal aggression to other pupils and to staff. The most recent incident resulted in her running out of class. Transition information from her previous school suggests that she was a very able student who made a positive contribution to classroom activities. Yvonne's attempts to engage with Sophie were challenging. She felt there was something going on but Sophie didn't want to talk about it.

Reflection

This situation is one which many teachers come across, and can appear very difficult to deal with. Yvonne's feeling of helplessness and isolation were compounded when, on asking a colleague how she might deal with Sophie's behaviour and what seemed like obvious external problems, she was told *their problems are nothing to do with me... I'm there to teach*. It is not easy to admit that you are having difficulty with the pupils you teach, and perhaps even less easy, if you feel there is no source of support for you.

Action Point

With a colleague, or with your mentor, discuss the possibilities open to Yvonne to support her with this dilemma. What are Yvonne's roles and responsibilities in relation to this situation? Who do you think she might talk to? What role might there be for in-class support for Sophie, and how might Yvonne manage that new relationship in her classroom? What ethical issues would she need to be aware of? What are the possible implications of Sophie disclosing something of a sensitive nature?

Stop and Read

Campbell, A. and Fairbairn, G. (2005) *Working with Support in the Classroom*. London: Paul Chapman Publishing.

This book uses case studies and stories to explore many of the issues and challenges of working with others to support learning in the classroom.

DfES (2000) *Working with Teaching Assistants: A good practice guide*. London: DfES.

A UK government guide to the role of the teaching assistant and how to develop effective partnership working with TAs.

Vincett, K., Cremin, H. and Thomas, G. (2005) *Teachers and Assistants Working Together*. Maidenhead: Open University Press/McGraw-Hill.

Based on research, this book examines models of collaborative classroom practice and provides practical tools for using the models, professional development and researching of this area of practice.

Case Study

Yvonne thinks about collaborating with others around and beyond the school
It was only when Yvonne mentioned contacting Sophie's mother that Sophie began to talk nervously. Her mother is a single parent and has not been well. Because of this Sophie is 'helping out' with the care for her mother and her two younger brothers. Keeping up with homework is a problem and she is 'a bit tired' in class. She doesn't want her mother to be contacted for fear of worrying her, nor does she want anyone else to help because she is worried what other people will think.

Yvonne is concerned with this situation and realises that she must speak to other colleagues. She is concerned that Sophie is quickly falling behind and wants to look at ways to help but is not presently sure what is available.

The diversified school workforce

As we have already seen, the context in which teaching takes place, at school level and across the wider field of work with children and young people, is changing. With Extended Schools and the emerging Twenty-first century School agenda we are likely to see the numbers and types of practitioners working in and around school change significantly.

The school workforce has, however, already diversified and it is commonplace to see the following staff within schools (in addition to those roles previously discussed) such as:

- bursars;
- administrators;
- business managers;
- extended services/schools co-ordinators.

Many of these roles support the day-to-day activities of 'traditional' school life, for example, finance and funding, maintaining student records or co-ordinating and administering processes such as timetables, teaching cover and registers. Increasingly, the roles involve the support and development of a range of services and initiatives that are linked to the school. This may include breakfast and after-school clubs, maintaining partnership with Early Years providers in the delivery of wraparound care, overseeing the use of the school for other services, organisations and activities, or securing large-scale funding for multi-agency delivery. A range of other staff, such as teaching assistants, Early Years workers, leisure workers, nursery nurses and catering staff may also work in this type of extended provision, possibly employed by the school.

In addition to these roles, a wide range of other practitioners may work within or around the school setting, including the following.

Educational psychologists assess the educational needs of children and provide advice on how these needs should be met, either at an individual/classroom level or across the whole school. They are also likely to provide other specific support for children and training for staff, working closely with the school's designated Special Educational Needs Co-ordinator (SENCO).

Speech and language therapists work with children, parents, carers and schools to assess and develop treatment and responses to speech and communication problems. They can work collaboratively with teachers, both inside and outside the classroom, to ensure that the needs of children with speech and language difficulties are most effectively met.

School nurses have a broad 'public health' function, seeking to ensure and promote the health and well-being of children and young people in areas such as obesity, sexual health, emotional health, smoking, drugs and alcohol. School nurses can provide a range of services and resources for children and schools (including support for classroom activity), as well as providing a different perspective into welfare and well-being issues within the school environment.

Connexions advisers provide information, advice and guidance for young people aged 11–19, primarily in the areas of education, careers, training and employment. In many areas they form part of an integrated youth support service, working with youth workers in a range of settings, including information centres, youth centres and schools.

Youth workers provide social activity and support with a focus on informal education. In a role that is not solely about leisure provision, youth workers seek to build relationships with young people, support their active participation and voice in issues affecting them, and promote their personal, spiritual and emotional well-being.

Education welfare officers (EWOs) work with schools and families to resolve attendance issues. The EWO has certain powers to enforce attendance at school through school attendance orders or other mechanisms. In many areas this role has been devolved to schools or in part taken up by others, for example with Police Community Support Officers (PCSOs) undertaking truancy patrols.

Counsellors. Employed either by the school or by external services (such as the voluntary sector, Primary Care Trust or the Child and Adolescent Mental Health Services (CAMHS), counsellors can offer confidential mental health support for children and young people.

Police Community Support Officers. Increasingly frequent within schools due to 'safer schools partnerships' and as part of some 'behaviour improvement programmes', police can be located in schools to reduce crime and anti-social behaviour around the school, reduce truancy, work with those at risk of getting involved in crime and support school staff in relation to crime and anti-social behaviour.

Leisure services may provide a range of activities within or around the school. They may also deliver class-based sessions in areas such as healthy eating or keep fit.

Specialist services and roles that can support schools to provide both education and welfare services also include substance misuse workers, dieticians, sexual health nurses, fire services and other professionals.

Much of this collaborative activity takes place through identified staff: head teachers, deputy or assistant heads, SENCOs, the designated child protection officer, extended schools co-ordinators or similar staff. Some teaching staff will, however, have more contact with these practitioners and the organisations they represent. Those working in special schools, for example, are much more likely to come into direct contact with the often complex web of professional services on a regular basis. Many of those within their care will receive support from such services and liaison and communication in order to ensure that the needs of the child are being met in a 'joined-up' way is more likely to be commonplace.

Working with other agencies and professionals in and beyond the school

In addition to the roles already described above, other agencies with a concern for the well-being of the child, and with a role that brings them into the domain of children's services, include youth justice workers (YOT staff), social workers, the police, other health practitioners (including GPs) and a wide range of voluntary and private-sector service providers.

For schools, much of the contact with these agencies comes either through collaborative activities within and around the school (for example nursery schools) or through making referrals when there are concerns about an individual's welfare or behaviour. The Common Assessment Framework (CAF) is a tool to draw together services to meet the needs of children and young people in an integrated way. It does not necessarily replace existing assessments (such as child protection risk assessments) but is intended for use when agencies (including schools) or parents identify a child or young person who would benefit from a 'joined-up' response from services to assist them to overcome barriers to learning or development. The tool is intended to promote 'swift and easy access' to child and adolescent mental health services (CAMHS), disability or special educational needs services. Following a CAF, in most areas a multi-agency panel brings together key services to examine how they can best meet the needs of the child. A lead professional is identified to co-ordinate this 'joined-up' response. A designated school lead or individual teacher may be invited to participate in this panel. In circumstances where action is required by a number of agencies, a 'team around the child' emerges to co-ordinate the response.

The approach relies on teachers (and other staff) being aware of their role in identifying emerging needs before they become large problems (early intervention) as well as in safeguarding the well-being of the child or young person. Teachers and other staff benefit from knowing what services may be able to help the child and also who is on hand within the school to discuss or support action based upon any emerging issues or concerns. In many schools this is likely to be the designated child protection officer, but the head teacher or other support staff may also fulfil this or similar functions.

It is important to distinguish between concerns about a child's progress or development (where they might benefit from a CAF) and situations that require immediate referrals to social services in order to safeguard the well-being of the child (for example, in the event of suspected abuse). Guidance should be available from schools for what to do in these circumstances and it is important that the appropriate person is informed of any concerns in this regard.

The increasing role of parents

While we have discussed at some length the various roles of professionals and agencies, we should also consider the growing role that parents play in the life of schools. Quite clearly parents have always played a significant part in the learning experiences of children and their engagement with school. A recent government report drawing together research in this area highlighted the impact of parental involvement in education, identifying the positive effect of involvement on achievement (DCSF, 2008d). The document also reported that while many parents reported being at least fairly involved in their child's education, two-thirds wanted to become more involved, though work commitments and childcare often stood in their way.

With the introduction of the Children's Plan (DCSF, 2007a) and the Twenty-first century School, the role of parents within and around school has been given greater prominence through the drive to encourage more extensive and effective work with parents and to support them *as partners in their child's learning* (DCSF, 2008c). This should, on the whole, be treated as a whole-school challenge, with consideration of initiatives like parent forums. There are, however, opportunities for teachers to consider and develop the contribution of parents when planning personalised learning. This is clearly not always easy since parental engagement with the teacher or school will vary considerably. However, a sensitivity to parents' concerns, awareness of literacy, numeracy and language issues and an approach to homework and other learning that seeks to create 'family learning' opportunities may well contribute to higher levels of parental involvement and increased attainment. Ultimately, teachers cannot force parents to become involved in the school or their children's learning. They may, however, through appropriate communication and learning activities which involve parents, be able to play a role in breaking down some of the barriers that prevent reluctant parents engaging with schools.

Reflection

Yvonne is beginning to realise that the help and support Sophie needs may have to come from other professionals as well as from a number of staff within the school. How can she go about accessing this support from outside the school?

Action Point

Discuss the following points with your MTL colleagues and with your mentor. Make sure that you know what is available in your school, and the structures and procedures for accessing this type of support.

- How much do you know about the roles of others within and around your school?
- How might other services help you in support of your learning role?
- What do you do if you have concerns about a child or young person? Are you aware of the support systems existing within the school?
- Talk to your SENCO or designated child protection officer about their role, the CAF and their relationship with other agencies. Are the new processes making a difference to children and young people?
- Think about what you need to help you better respond to the emerging needs of children in your class and to identify safeguarding issues.

Stop and Read

Cheminais, R. (2006) *Every Child Matters: A Practical Guide for Teachers*. London: Sage.
    A practical overview of the implications of Every Child Matters for teachers and schools. Other information for SENCOs and teaching assistants is also available.
Cheminais, R. (2009) *Effective Multi-Agency Partnerships: Putting Every Child Matters into Practice*. London: Sage.
    An exploration of what it means to develop effective multi-agency working, managing and working within multi-agency settings and evaluating the impact of partnership work.
Fitzgerald, D. and Kay, J. (2008) *Working Together in Children's Services*. Abingdon: Routledge.
    This book provides an explanation of what it means to 'work together', as well as an overview of children's services, the CAF and lead professional role. It also examines some of the barriers to, and skills needed for, integrated working.

Walker, G. (2008) *Working Together for Children: A critical introduction to multi-agency working*. London: Continuum.
An overview and analysis of the processes of working together (such as safeguarding and information sharing) and the role of, among others, schools and parents.

Key strategies for developing this content area

Becoming familiar with principles of working with other professionals in a multi-agency approach will take some time. Some of the key ideas to help you get to grips with this are discussed below, and we then complete this section with an illustration of how one teacher, Donna, used her own practice as SENCO as the basis of a case study approach to further enhance her practice in this respect.

Principles and practice of multi-agency working and collaborative practice

Working with other agencies and professional groups can bring about many benefits, both for children and for practitioners. Cheminais (2009) identifies a range of benefits, including:

- improved awareness of other services and signposting to support services can enable teachers to concentrate more effectively on their core role;
- the promotion of mutual support, encouragement and the exchange of ideas between staff;
- the development of broader perspectives on situations;
- a greater ability to plan, bid for and deliver collaborative services and projects that could not be delivered alone;
- the ability to see others' perspectives and agency issues and to break down professional boundaries and parochial attitudes.

There can be a wide range of challenges, too. Other agencies may not always do what we expect of them or services might be driven by competing demands, targets or priorities. Different professional groups may also operate in different cultures, use different terminology, and age-old prejudices and assumptions about services or groups can serve to inhibit integrated or collaborative practice. These issues can sometimes be overcome by spending focused time working alongside or in conversation with professionals from other agencies. Indeed, much positive collaborative practice evolves in this way, with individuals from different professions identifying common principles and values and seeking to work together. Work with other professionals can also enable us to see our own world and practice through a new lens. With different training and, for example, a different way of seeing the child and child development, we may be able to gain insights into new ways of delivering personalised learning to particular groups or individuals. We can also contribute to others' greater understanding of the role of education and the teacher.

Time, and the opportunity for dialogue among other professional groups, is often something of a luxury and is rarely available to us. Because of this there is a risk that we get stuck in our own professional ways of working without considering the contribution others can make to our own teaching and to the well-being of pupils. Our contact with other agencies then becomes infrequent and when it does take place, all groups may be suspicious, have unrealistic expectations of one another, based upon lack of understanding, or even be hostile or antagonistic.

Whether working with colleagues in the classroom or agencies from outside school, there are, however, a set of skills and attributes that can assist us in our work with others, whether in the classroom, with parents or with other agencies. Drawing from Anning *et al.* (2006), Cheminais (2006, 2009), DfES (2005a), Fitzgerald and Kay (2008) and Walker and Thurston (2006), these include:

- have a shared vision, purpose or common goal for the piece of collaborative work (in the interests of the child or young person);
- be an open and honest communicator;
- trust others and respect their professional (or para-professional) role;
- be willing to listen to and understand different perspectives;
- be willing to compromise, where appropriate, in the interests of the common goal;
- have a clear sense of your own professional role and perspective (while valuing the role of others);
- trust your own professional judgements;
- avoid making assumptions;
- be willing to question and discuss terminology and differences in language and concepts, while also seeking to communicate in a clear way to others.

Essentially, many of these skills and abilities are underpinned by the core aspects of the MTL: reflective practice and critical analysis. A critically reflective teacher is able to consider and develop their own practice in the context of different and sometimes conflicting evidence and perspectives, questioning assumptions about their own and others' practice as they learn and develop. The critically reflective teacher is also a capable communicator, able to describe and analyse their own professional practice in a clear and coherent manner to a variety of audiences. Thus, the above skills should be seen as central to the role of a professional teacher and not skills solely for multi-agency working. This does not mean that we should automatically assume that we possess such skills, however. We need to be constantly reflective about our ability to work with others, whether in the classroom or beyond, in order to continue to develop high-quality teaching and learning opportunities for children and young people.

Chapter 1 provides support for you in turning research data from your practice into a reflective case study, which both serves to help you deepen your understanding of practice, and also, should have a positive impact on it. Donna's story provides a framework for this which you might like to emulate.

Case Study

Donna is the SENCO in a medium-sized primary school on the outskirts of a large conurbation. For her, multi-agency work is commonplace, though not without frustrations. She feels that she has an ever-increasing role but is often dependent on the services of outside agencies such as educational psychologists, Child and Adolescent Mental Health Services (CAMHS) and social workers to support her. Such services tend to offer general advice but little in the way of direct services and they are difficult to co-ordinate in the interest of the child. Sometimes she doesn't really understand their role or 'where they are coming from'. Following a local authority training session, she is now being encouraged to complete a CAF for some pupils and to convene multi-agency groups. Changes to the local Children's Trust structure and the devolution of the local Education Welfare Service mean that she has found it increasingly difficult to get support and she is worried that the CAF is yet another burden to her practice. She is positive about the vision for the CAF and integrated working but is unsure whether it will actually improve anything for the school or the child. She is interested in finding out more about multi-agency working and the role of others to enable her to get the best for the children with whom she works.

For her phase 3 study Donna is undertaking a case study of the school's approach to multi-agency working and the responses of services working with the school. She interviews key staff within the school and also agencies working with and around the school to find out their perspectives on multi-agency working and the school's role in relation to this. She analyses this information and sets it in context of the Twenty-first century school vision, highlighting some of the different perspectives at play in relation to how the school is seen and sees others. Her conclusions form the basis of a personal and organisational action plan for improved collaboration between the school and other agencies in the area.

Assignments

Suggested assignments to address this content area

- Undertake one of the psychometric assessment exercises mentioned at the start of the chapter (or use any other instrument you are familiar with/have access to). Prepare a PowerPoint presentation for your MTL colleagues explaining the nature of the assessment, and suggesting ways in which it could be used to provide a strategic insight into leadership development planning.
- Conduct a formal interview with a leader in your school or setting. Use the analysis of the interview to help you understand the challenges and opportunities of leadership, and the ways in which you can best prepare yourself for taking on such responsibility. Write up the interview, and annotate it with learning points (using theoretical perspectives to help you develop and deepen your understanding).
- Construct a SWOT analysis of multi-agency or integrated working for your situation. Present a report of the analysis, and some recommendations for practice.

- Consider and reflect on your experiences of working with other professional groups. What factors made these experiences positive or negative? Prepare a brief report to present to a group of colleagues.
- Explore the opportunities that are there for you to develop your understanding and skills in work with others. How might you make best use of such opportunities? Draw up an annotated action plan, indicating what learning resources will help you at each stage. What professional development opportunities will you need to avail yourself of?
- Conduct a survey of the contemporary literature (books, journals and acceptable web-based materials) on some particular aspect of leadership or collaborative practice that you are interested in. Write up a review, extracting key themes and issues.
- If you already have a leadership or collaborative practice responsibility, write a philosophy of practice statement. Then, over a period of time, keep a reflective diary (if possible, ask some colleagues to observe you and also keep diaries which they will share with you). When you have kept your reflective diary for a few weeks, compare your actual practice to your personal philosophy of practice. Are there areas of similarity? Difference? Attempt to explain analytically any difference you have uncovered.
- Choose one of the theoretical frameworks from the literature, and assess the extent to which your style and practice reflect that.

Summary

At the end of this chapter you should have:
- begun to understand how your own leadership capacity might be developed;
- an awareness of a range of leadership concepts, and an understanding of their applicability in your own context;
- an understanding of some of the tools available to facilitate self-assessment in relation to teamwork and leadership;
- developed a greater understanding of integrated and multi-agency and team working and be able to identify your own and the school's role within this context;
- a greater understanding of the professionals and services available to children and young people and be able to identify ways to identify structures and individual contacts (within and outside your school) to support children with additional needs;
- a greater awareness of the skills and knowledge required to work in an integrated way with other practitioners and be able to identify personal learning needs in this area.

Further reading

Bennis, W. and Goldsmith, J. (1997) *Learning to Lead*. London: Nicholas Brealey.

Brighouse, T. and Woods, D. (1999) *How to Improve your School*. Abingdon: Routledge.

Earley, P. and Weindling, D. 2004 *Understanding School Leadership*. London: Paul Chapman Publishing.

Useful websites

Every Child Matters **www.everychildmatters.gov.uk**

Children's Workforce Development Council (CWDC) **www.cwdcouncil.org.uk**

National College for School Leadership (NCSL) **www.ncsl.org.uk**

Training and Development Agency for Schools (TDA) **www.tda.gov.uk**

PART THREE

PHASE 3: DEEPENING

CHAPTER 7

Phase 3: The final phase

What is important is to keep learning, to enjoy challenge, and to tolerate ambiguity. In the end there are no certain answers.

(Martina Horner, President of Radcliffe College, 1960s)

Chapter Objectives

This chapter, written in two sections, will guide you in the final stages of your MTL by providing you with:

- a systematic understanding of how to access, interpret, use and apply research, national frameworks and practical knowledge in relation to your specialist field, in order to help you improve your practice;
- support to communicate clearly your conclusions to specialist and non-specialist audiences in your school and beyond;
- ideas for engaging in collaborative learning opportunities in your specialist professional field and through planning for further professional development;
- support to act autonomously in planning and implementing tasks at a professional level, and undertake problem-solving in practice;
- support to design, carry out and critically analyse a master's-level, practice-based enquiry in your specialist professional field, which explores relationships between theoretical and practical knowledge, and impacts on practice;
- support to make sound judgements on complex issues, even when evidence is incomplete.

In this final phase of your MTL, you will be starting to draw together the academic skills, the practical wisdom, and the academic and practical knowledge you have been developing in the first two phases. To date, you have had opportunities for developing your knowledge in the four content areas, for testing out some ideas in your practice, for being mentored and coached by more experienced colleagues, and for being introduced to a range of academic skills and processes. Now you can start a more independent approach to your learning.

Links to the professional standards
Depending on the specific focus of the work you undertake at this stage of your studies, you will link to different standards. However, in terms of the generic skills and attributes you will be addressing, the following are central.

Personal professional development
C7, C8, C9

Reviewing teaching and learning
C35

Team working and collaboration
C40

This chapter deals with phase 3, the last stage of your MTL, and the stage in which you consolidate what you have learned in the previous two phases. Through developing your subject knowledge, and pedagogy and practice, you are in a position to substantially deepen your understanding of what it is to be a good teacher. This phase involves two elements, each worth 30 credits, which will provide you with opportunities to develop your knowledge, and demonstrate excellence in your practice.

In this chapter, we will look at ways in which you can complete the assessment tasks for the last two elements, and also provide some support for the higher-level skills you will be expected to demonstrate at this stage.

Section 1: Drawing on leading-edge expertise

In this section, we will explore ways in which you can access leading-edge expertise, and provide support for the skills needed to enable you to make best use of it.

What do we mean by leading-edge expertise? A useful starting point is the Leading Edge Partnership Programme, established in 2003 and now aligned with the Specialist Schools programme since 2005. The programme is about secondary schools working together to address some of the most critical learning challenges facing the education system. The key focus of the programme was to support the raising-achievement agenda, and develop networks of best practice, and the partnership intends to publish case studies of effective networking both on the Leading Edge site (**www.ledge.org.uk**) and also in hard copy. This one source of information provides practice-based resources and evidence relating to work to raise achievement in schools. Connecting with such a network may provide you with opportunities to undertake some of the professional development activities discussed below. There are other ways in which you can access first-class theoretical and practical knowledge, and undertake activities which will enhance and deepen your own knowledge, understanding and practice.

Let us explore three important ways in which you can engage with specialist expertise, the review of existing literature and research, collaborative working with subject associations or other sources of expertise, and having the opportunity to shadow an expert at work. Each of these three methods will be discussed under three headings: skills required, advantages, disadvantages.

Reviewing existing literature and research

Skills required

This is an important academic skill, and one which also can have a very strong positive impact on your own professional development. It underpins much of the work that you will undertake at this final stage of your MTL. Also, it is the skill that at this stage you are most likely to require high-level support in. For these reasons, it will form the biggest 'skills required' section of the three approaches.

First of all it is important to decide the focus of your literature review. Having too broad a focus is a common problem in carrying out research, and before you start, you need to be aware of the limitations on your time and resources, and also to be aware of the fact that without a clear focus, you will be unlikely to have a focused report, and hence the report may be of little use to you. The purpose of reviewing literature and existing research is to find out what is already known about a topic or subject, and if necessary, to comment on it. Ridley (2008) discusses the term 'literature review' as both a process (of reviewing the literature) and a product (the written end report), and suggests that conducting a literature review is a continuous process throughout research, informing the analysis of primary research findings, and guiding the research as it progresses. However, at this stage we will focus simply on the concept of a literature review as a process (and product) for developing knowledge and understanding in a chosen specialist field. This review may be to help you plan some primary research of your own, or it may be to inform you about what is already known, in order to improve your own knowledge and understanding. Undertaking a literature review has three basic parts to it.

1. Clarifying the focus for the review.
2. Finding and reading the relevant literature and research publications.
3. Preparing the final review.

Let us look first of all at clarifying the focus. This important first step should not be over-looked, or treated lightly. The success of the review depends on this initial clarity: there really is a lot of wisdom in the old proverb *Well begun is half done*. Consider the situation of a teacher wishing to do some research on what has been published about the effective teaching of science. If she searches online for 'effective science teaching', she will find over 26,000 results in a simple internet search. If she goes to the library looking for information on effective science teaching, it is likely that the librarian will ask her to be more specific. Details such as age range, type of school, locality/context and so on, will all point to different resources. In order to make the search manageable and useful for her, whether she searches online or in a library, she will need to start putting some parameters or boundaries on her search. It may be for example that she wants to find out about teaching a particular aspect of the science curriculum, say 'Materials and their properties', to Year 8 children in a rural comprehensive school. This will immediately limit the scope of her study. However, if we look again at her initial question, it is important to understand what she means by 'effective' teaching. This could mean teaching that motivates children, and is enjoyable for them, or teaching that a teacher, and perhaps a reviewer, feel to be effective, or it may be about the type of teaching that seems to produce best outcomes in terms of pupil achievement. Without clarifying what is meant by the wording of the question, as well as its scope, she really does not have a feasible research question. Once some thought has been given to getting a clear and manageable focus, it is time to consider where the source materials can be found.

While there is no denying the way in which the internet has made resources available to us in a convenient way, when it comes to finding and reading the relevant literature and research, a visit to a library is often the best place to start. As a student on MTL, you will already be a member of your university library. If you have not already done so, it is worthwhile to ask a librarian to show you how to search the numerous databases and electronic resources, as well as books, other publications and media. Burton and Bartlett (2009) provide a useful and succinct overview of conducting a library search in Chapter 5 of their book. Rae Stark's paper (1998) provides an accessible set of guidelines for conducting a literature review, and includes a particularly useful 'How not to' section, and like other texts, includes some guidance on making sure that you keep accurate references of the materials you have read. As you begin your reading, you may begin to see themes emerging, and this will help you to do two things. In the first instance, the structure from these themes will help to organise your reading and your follow-up reading. As you read, you can find that you seem to be in a never-ending spiral of increasing complexity, as one text leads to another (slightly different, but interesting) one. Having an identified set of themes from your early reading can help you guide your reading more strategically, and prevent you branching out too far and getting sidetracked. Secondly, the themes you identify (although you will probably refine them as you continue to read) can help form a structure for the final report.

In terms of preparing the final review, Harlen and Schlapp (1998) suggest ways of structuring the write-up of the literature review, relating the sections to those normally found in an empirical report: *an introduction, a 'methods' section indicating how and why the studies included in the review were selected, the main body of the review, and a conclusion.* The themes you have identified can be used then to structure the main body of the review. A literature review such as this is normally a discursive piece of writing, and you should try to avoid making it into a 'what I have read' list, instead relating it to the focus of your own research, and providing a critical analysis and overview. An alternative to the formal literature review is the annotated bibliography. This is similar in purpose to a literature review, but different in structure. It may be that your task requires you to review the literature, and use that review to develop your own knowledge and understanding, but that the format of the assignment task is not specified. If this is the case, you might find the annotated bibliography a useful way of presenting this. You should still use themes, but the work is generally presented as a series of commentaries on the texts you have read, to which you can provide an overall introduction and conclusion. You can decide on the nature of the commentary needed to suit your task. Whichever format you choose, reading critically is central, and you may recall the reference, in Chapter 2, to the work of Poulson and Wallace (2004) on becoming a critical reader (and writer). The list they provide of the attributes is a useful starting place in reviewing research reports, articles and texts.

If you do decide to produce an annotated bibliography, the following guidelines, adapted from materials available at the University of Wisconsin's Writing Center, may be helpful if you decide to use this type of presentation.

1. Introductory paragraph indicating the purpose and scope of the piece.
2. Choose the citation style you will use. Harvard is used in many UK education faculties. You will need to cite the text you are commenting on in the appropriate style.
3. Write your review of the text using the following criteria as appropriate.
   - Explanation of the main points or purpose of the work.
   - Perspective of the author and the audience the text was written for.
   - Links to other work in the area.
   - Evaluation of the source or author critically (biases, lack of evidence, objective, etc.).
   - Indication of how the work may or may not be useful for a particular field of study or audience.
   - Relationship of this text to your question or focus.
4. A summary paragraph indicating how the overall piece has informed your knowledge and understanding in relation to your research question or focus.

The open-source site at Purdue University Online Writing Lab (OWL), provides a wide range of tutorials and samples of work to assist in your writing. The following example of an excerpt from an annotated bibliography is taken from there, and uses a citation style known as Modern Languages Association (MLA). While this is not likely to be the citation style you will need to use, the example nonetheless is very helpful.

Lamott, Anne. Bird by Bird: Some Instructions on Writing and Life. New York: Anchor Books, 1995. Print.

Lamott's book offers honest advice on the nature of a writing life, complete with its insecurities and failures. Taking a humorous approach to the realities of being a writer, the chapters in Lamott's book are wry and anecdotal and offer advice on everything from plot development to jealousy, from perfectionism to struggling with one's own internal critic. In the process, Lamott includes writing exercises designed to be both productive and fun.

Lamott offers sane advice for those struggling with the anxieties of writing, but her main project seems to be offering the reader a reality check regarding writing, publishing, and struggling with one's own imperfect humanity in the process. Rather than a practical handbook to producing and/or publishing, this text is indispensable because of its honest perspective, its down-to-earth humor, and its encouraging approach.

Chapters in this text could easily be included in the curriculum for a writing class. Several of the chapters in Part 1 address the writing process and would serve to generate discussion on students' own drafting and revising processes. Some of the writing exercises would also be appropriate for generating classroom writing exercises. Students should find Lamott's style both engaging and enjoyable.

In the sample annotation above, the writer includes three paragraphs: a summary, an evaluation of the text, and a reflection on its applicability to his/her own research, respectively.

(http://owl.english.purdue.edu/owl/resource/614/03/)

Advantages of reviewing literature and research

As a teacher in a rapidly changing world, it is imperative that you keep abreast of current developments in education. Conducting a review of contemporary literature and research gives you access to cutting-edge knowledge in your field, and encourages you to gain a broader perspective than you might otherwise gain. Producing a review of the literature also is a tangible way for you to demonstrate your own knowledge of the field, and allows you to draw from this to inform your professional dialogue, knowing that you can support your argument and claims, and also to inform your practice in a way that is research-informed. It also allows you to communicate your knowledge effectively to others. This may be through a discursive review, where readers can see the validity and strength of your claims, and may decide to follow up on some of the materials you have cited, or it may be through the annotated bibliography where you provide very specific information and guidance on a range of sources. It will allow others to make well-informed choices about texts they might wish to read, or that they might find useful. There are many other personal benefits too, in that as a professional, you become accustomed to the way in which professional and academic reports and reviews are written, and in developing such familiarity, become better placed to take a full part in your professional community of practice.

Disadvantages of reviewing literature and research

There are few, if any disadvantages with becoming familiar with research and literature in your field. If one had to level any complaint against the literature review, it would probably be at it as a sole stimulus for professional learning. There are some schools of thought that suggest that with such an 'ivory towers' approach, much practical knowledge is overlooked. However, if you are aware of the range of different types of research reports and literature available, you will be able to make sure that you also include some practice-based reports. You will see that in fact many journal articles, especially ones in journals like *Educational Action Research* and the *Journal of Reflective Practice* are written by practitioners, and are accounts of their own professional learning and development.

Collaborative working with subject associations or other sources of expertise

Skills required

As before, it is important to get a starting point when you wish to develop some specific expertise. The clearer this is, the better you can engage with the resource or opportunity. Working with a subject association can be a very effective way of enhancing your subject-based knowledge, and the case study in Chapter 4 shows you how Laura effectively undertook some collaborative working with a subject association in order to enhance her subject knowledge. This type of working can also be used in order to produce the type of formal report that could be used as part of a phase 3 MTL assessment. In order to make best use of this type of collaboration, you need to plan at the start exactly what you will do, and how you will record it. Will you, for example, use the expertise in the association to help in the development of cutting-edge teaching and learning resources for your own class, and others? Will you perhaps write a reflective report, outline your own professional learning through the work with the association? Perhaps you would prefer to keep a portfolio of evidence of your learning? Might you perhaps decide to run an in-service event for colleagues, or an information evening for parents, or governors, and prepare a presentation and supporting handout materials? In each of these cases, you need to be clear at the outset not just what your focus is, but also the purpose of your work. You can then plan what type of materials and resources to build up during the collaborative work, and as you go along, you can be assessing their suitability for your final report. If you decide to keep a portfolio of your learning, you will need to decide how it will be structured, and how you will select the most appropriate evidence for inclusion in each section. Your HEI tutor will be able to give you advice about that, and guide you to some supportive reading materials. As a starting point, you might find 'Using portfolios in the assessment of learning and competence: the impact of four models', by Endacott *et al.* (2004) helpful. Although written about nurse education, it deals with the needs of professional practice-based learners, and can easily be applied to similar work in education.

Another source of expertise that you might consider, or have made available to you, is the opportunity to work with a local INSET provider, perhaps on a period of secondment. This can be an extremely valuable opportunity not only to work with a team of experts, but also to get a chance to work in a range of other schools and settings, most of which will be different to your own. If you do get such an opportunity, view it as a significant learning experience. You could consider keeping a learning journal as evidence of your professional development, and using an edited version of it as a phase 3 assignment.

An opportunity exists at times in some universities to become a research associate, and either working with members of an academic research team, or undertaking some supported practice-based research yourself. This will give you access to people who have significant practice-based experience, and also high levels of academic expertise. If you are offered, and allowed to avail yourself of such an opportunity, you could focus your work on something that is important to you in your own practice, and use that as the focus of your research report. Again, this could form the basis of a phase three MTL assignment.

Advantages of collaborative working with subject associations or other sources of expertise

In each of the examples above, and indeed in any other forms of collaborative working that you may undertake, a key advantage is the potential for forming ongoing networking opportunities. Seeing the world beyond your own classroom, school or setting is perhaps one of the best experiences a teacher can have. Even if the degree of match between your new opportunity and your normal practice is not perfect, there can still be much to learn. The case study at the end of this section (my own story) illustrates an example of professional learning from working in a different setting.

Disadvantages of collaborative working with subject associations or other sources of expertise

Working collaboratively is almost always beneficial, not least for the networking opportunities it gives you. However, as in any collaborative venture, it is possible that your own aims can be overlooked by others in the collaboration. While there may be some need for you to renegotiate your own initial aims (and remember, they may very much need rethinking, and an outside opinion can be just what's needed), you do need to be careful that your willingness to work is not being hijacked to suit someone else's ends.

Shadow an expert at work

Skills required

This can take one of two forms. Either you simply shadow, and observe the work of someone who is more experienced and expert than you and from that, perhaps compile a report, or analysis of their work, or you observe in an 'apprenticeship' way, sometimes known as 'sitting by Nelly', and as a result of that try to emulate their work in order to improve your own.

Whether your shadowing opportunity is of the first or second type, a valuable skill for you to develop is the skill of focused and formal observation. In a way, this may echo some experiences and opportunities you had as a trainee teacher, where some of your placement time was spent watching the classes of more experienced teachers. You will probably have found this a very rich and valuable experience. At this stage in your career, you might have an opportunity to observe someone working in a different professional area, which would help you in developing your understanding of the multi-agency context in which schools now exist. Alternatively, you might develop your understanding and leadership capacity by shadowing someone in a senior leadership position. In either case, you need to prepare yourself well in order to optimise the observation opportunity. In many ways, it is possible to underestimate the extent to which we need to prepare carefully to observe others at work, since it seems like such an intuitive part of what we do as teachers, and indeed, in ordinary, everyday, non-professional life. Burton and Bartlett (2009) however, devote a full chapter to it in their book, emphasising the importance of this skill in education research, and provide a useful set of guidelines and observation schedules to suit a range of different situations. As in any other research activity, the most important thing is to get a clear starting point, deciding exactly what you hope to gain from the experience. Once you have done this, you are in a position to select an already designed observation schedule, or to customise one to suit your own needs, or develop your own. Many teachers choose to either customise or develop their own, recognising the complexity of education in context, and the important, but subtle, differences which exist between two seemingly similar situations. It is a good idea to try out some practice formal observations before you actually undertake the ones that you hope to base a report on, so that you can pilot the schedule you have developed, and also, to find out how you can cope with both observing and recording your observations at the same time. Piloting the session can also help the person you are observing to be more at ease, and hence, more natural in their behaviour, which is what you will be hoping for. You should also consider keeping a research diary as a supplementary activity to formal observations, as you will be able to use that to note other, perhaps unexpected, but significant events. This can actually refocus your shadowing activity, and suggest an amendment to the observation schedule.

Advantages of shadowing an expert at work

Watching people in their work has a number of key strengths. In particular, we can see how people actually do go about their job, or behave in particular situations. A common perceived weakness of interviews and questionnaires is that people may overestimate their 'good' qualities or behaviours, and underestimate their 'bad' ones. Observing people allows you to see what they actually do, rather than what they say they do. Also, if planned properly, they can help you see, through observing other practice, how you can better reflect on or develop your own. If you are observing in a 'sitting by Nelly' capacity with a view to specifically learning new skills, then there is a an advantage also for the person that you are observing if they help you by articulating their professional knowledge in practice.

Disadvantages of shadowing an expert at work

Depending on what you want to observe, it may be difficult to gain access. Like all research, you are always dependent on the goodwill and co-operation of others, and many people may feel reticent about letting you into their private space in this capacity. At other times, in particular for example, if you are observing a senior manager at work, the nature of the work may involve some sensitive and confidential discussions that you would not be allowed to observe. It is also possible that the person you are observing may be so conscious of your presence that their behaviour changes because of that, and so what you see is not an accurate picture of their practice.

Reflection

Consider a situation where you have the opportunity to shadow the work of someone from another professional background who is also working with children and young people. How might you select who you want to observe, and why? Discuss with your colleagues and your coach and tutor how you might go about obtaining permission for this to happen, and what, if any limits there will be on the opportunity.

Action Point

Draw up an outline plan of the observation period taking into account the following questions.

- What is the focus of the observation?
- How many times will you want to observe them, and over what period?
- How will you record the observations?
- Will the observee be allowed to see any notes or report that you write?
- Is this an observation from which you hope to learn a practical skill? Or one in which you want to gain an insight into and understanding of some other practice?
- How will you present a final report?
- How will you ensure it is not judgmental?

It is worth remembering here, as in the other ways of engaging with current research and practice, that arriving at a conclusion is not always easy, as the evidence base may be incomplete. We will explore the nature and status of evidence in the next section.

Case Study

My own story of professional learning

After 16 years' teaching science and physics in A-level, I saw in the local paper an opportunity to apply for a seconded post to the local authority curriculum advisory service. This seemed like the perfect opportunity for me to rejuvenate my teaching, as the job entailed four days per week working in a number of schools, alongside teachers, helping them develop pedagogy, resources, and practice. I was also to work with teams in the schools on the writing of planning documents and policies. On the fifth day of each week, I was to work with the advisory team either planning or delivering INSET provision for teachers throughout the authority region. It was with some trepidation however, that I approached my head teacher to ask permission to apply for the seconded post. The reason for my trepidation was that the post was based in the primary sector, and as a secondary (mainly A-level) teacher, I was concerned that she would think the experience irrelevant. I was also concerned that I would not get past the shortlisting stage of the application because of this perceived mismatch.

However, I was lucky in that my head did see that this was potentially a valuable opportunity and one that I would benefit from. She felt that it would provide good networking opportunities, allow me to understand the science curriculum as it was in the primary sector, and would feed back into more effective continuity and transition planning on my return to my own job.

I was successful in the interview, and took up post with the authority primary science and technology team for a period of a year. During that year, I was studying as a PhD student part-time, and was keeping a reflective log as part of my ongoing research into the practice of contemporary science education. I recorded in my diary that I was surprised to find when working with small children that their response to concepts in science was often more emotional or aesthetically based than the responses of the older children I was used to teaching, and noted that *small children [were] describing, often with delight, the aesthetic features of these objects. They talked of the beautiful colour of flowers, their smell, their soft feel against the skin.* This was so different to my own experiences, but caused me to think very deeply about the way in which science in secondary school could possibly be losing its appeal to students, particularly in an all-girls school such as the one I taught at. My PhD had started by questioning why it was that fewer girls were choosing A-level physics than had previously, and my experience of working with the primary children gave me a completely different perspective on how the wonder of science could be perhaps lost with older students. The (at that time) removal of 'colour' from the Key Stages 3 and 4 curriculum meant that those students who had experience of mixing coloured lights (in drama, for example), or paints (in art) lost what many teachers at the time thought was a valuable, and aesthetically pleasing, aspect of the curriculum.

On my return to school the following year, I used my experiences to undertake some primary research in my school, canvassing views from the pupils about their perceptions of science and scientists, and their experiences of science education. Based on this research, I instigated a science club with the help of a local university student, bringing a range of extracurricular activities to as many students as possible. What started off as an opportunity to see other practice, turned into an experience that ultimately had a positive impact on my own practice.

Reflection

Discuss with your colleagues what types of opportunities you might be interested in, and find out how you might access them. What benefits do you think you could gain from a period of secondment or a work-shadowing opportunity? What type of report do you think would provide a record of your professional learning through this opportunity?

Section 2: Problem-solving in practice: an enquiry resulting in impact on learning

Often it is challenging enough to look critically at one's own teaching practices. While the obvious purpose of self-study is improvement, it is even more challenging to make changes and seek evidence that the changes did indeed represent improvement.

(Russell, 2002, pp3–4)

This element of your MTL offers you the opportunity for undertaking some practice-based research and evaluating its impact on learning. During earlier parts of your study, you have undertaken some elements of practitioner research, and should now have developed the skills of reflection, enquiry, academic reading and academic writing. In addition, during this last phase, you should also have become more familiar with academic and research literature.

The two key concepts to consider here are master's-level enquiry and impact on learning. In the first instance, you will be expected to demonstrate a good understanding of how to plan and undertake some academically sound research into practice which has been designed to impact on learning. Secondly, you will be expected to show that there is evidence of impact.

The list later in this chapter gives the main points you need to consider when embarking on a practitioner research project. Most of these points will have been dealt with in some degree in other parts of the book, but in undertaking a project like this, you will need to consider them all. As in other aspects of your work, getting a clear focus or starting point is important. You need to remember that this enquiry is one which is meant to demonstrate impact on pupil and colleague learning, and so your starting point should be developed with this in mind. You can do this by either deciding to evaluate some new curriculum initiative in your practice, perhaps something that has been developed during, or provided, at some in-service course you have attended, or you can, on the basis of some evidence about your own practice, develop some customised initiative of your own.

In undertaking both these tasks, you need to start by considering some important terminology and concepts. As Tom Russell's words at the start of this section suggest, the use of the word 'evidence' here is important, and one which we need to take some time to consider. It is a word that we frequently hear associated with practice: 'evidence-based practice', 'evidence-informed practice', and indeed, 'practice-based evidence'. As a word, evidence means 'that which proves or disproves something', and so we should use it carefully, and assess the extent to which our 'evidence' can actually support the claims that we make. Whitehead usefully distinguishes between 'data' and 'evidence':

I make a clear distinction between data and evidence. I am thinking of data as the information that is collected during an enquiry. I am thinking of evidence as data that is used to support or refute a belief, assertion, hypothesis or claim to knowledge.

(Whitehead, 2003)

Furthermore, writing for the Teacher Training Resource Bank, Richard Andrews supports, and augments this, by introducing us to the fact that evidence implies a particular set of values.

> *Data, for example, are not necessarily evidence and vice-versa. Data can take various forms but are inert unless they are informed by a claim, thesis or proposition. To use Toulmin's terminology (1958/2003), a claim is supported by grounds (evidence), the connection warranted by values and conventions within a field (e.g. a discipline). Evidence, therefore, is infused with ideas, assumptions and values. Data, relatively speaking, are not.*
>
> (Andrews, 2003)

As a teacher, you have access to very rich data sources. Your engagement with MTL, in particular at this stage, can help you use that data in a way that supports some claim you make, and hence, becomes the evidence for that claim. With a clear starting point for your enquiry, you can make informed choices about the types of data that you will select, and also decide how you will use them in support of the claim you make.

So, what type of data is available to you? Coe *et al.* (2000), suggest that *the 'gold-standard' of evidence is taken to be multiple replications of small scale, randomised controlled trials (RCT) of feasible interventions in real-life settings* (p2). This medical concept of 'evidence-based practice' is predicated on the concept of 'hard evidence', or propositional knowledge. However, even in medicine, this is challenged. Rycroft-Malone *et al.* (2004) suggest that the professional, tacit knowledge of practitioners is as important a part of the potential evidence-base as propositional knowledge. Although they are talking about the health practice setting, it can be seen how this clearly relates to education, in all its person-centred complexity.

> *However, this non-propositional knowledge has the potential to become propositional knowledge once it has been articulated by individual practitioners, then debated, contested and verified through wider communities of practice in the critical social science tradition of theory generation (see Titchen and Ersser 2001). In order to practise evidence-based, person-centred care, practitioners need to draw on and integrate multiple sources of propositional and non-propositional knowledge informed by a variety of evidence bases that have been critically and publicly scrutinized.*
>
> (Rycroft-Malone, *et al.*, 2003)

In reality, as a teacher, you have access to both propositional knowledge (in the form of externally- and internally-generated performance indicators, and other statistics), and non-propositional knowledge (in the form of interview transcripts, observations, focus group discussions, and so forth) about your practice.

Whitehead's work on self-study in teacher education practices (s-step) suggests five key questions to assist in an evidence-based enquiry.

1. *Is there evidence of the generation and testing of educational theories from the embodied knowledge of s-step researchers?*
2. *Is there evidence of the transformation of the embodied values of the s-step researcher into the standards of judgement that can be used to test the validity of s-step accounts?*
3. *Is there evidence of the emergence of educational research methodologies as distinct from a social science methodology in s-step enquiries?*
4. *Is there evidence of a logic of educational enquiry?*
5. *Is there evidence of educational influence in educating oneself, in the learning of others and in the education of social formations?*

(Whitehead, 2003)

Questions such as these, or your own adaptation of them could help you in deciding exactly which data you will use to evidence your claims, and will also challenge you to ensure that your enquiry has the academic rigour that master's-level demands, and also brings us to the next key concept, that of impact. Whitehead's last question indicates that our work must have some educational influence or impact.

Impact, like evidence, is also a word that is often used in different ways, and if we claim to have made an impact, then we need also to explain the nature and scope of that impact. The BBC news headline on their website in December 2008 'Behaviour classes "lack impact"', caused quite a stir suggesting that the high-profile Social and Emotional Aspects of Learning (SEAL) programme had not had the desired impact on behaviour. Commenting on the report, a DCSF spokesperson said that

> *SEAL is working well in many schools across the country, helping to tackle the causes of bad behaviour and bullying by helping all children to develop self-control and good relationships. Many schools that have implemented SEAL have seen a marked improvement in the way their pupils interact with each other both inside and outside the classroom.*

However, despite a 'general perception' that the programme had had a positive benefit on behaviour and school work, research undertaken by a team at Manchester University found little or no evidence to substantiate that claim.

On the other hand, an evaluation of the long-term impact of school trips as part of the National Trust Guardianship Scheme, suggested that there were many benefits, and that the impact was significant. Citing nine key benefits of participation on pupils and schools, the Trust does identify areas for improvement, but overall, assess the impact as

> *very apparent from this study and a range of others already referred to, that working outside the classroom on curriculum-related topics with expert adults has many tangible benefits for pupils across a wide range of age and attainment. Those benefits encompass attitudes to learning and related skills in particular, as well as to behaviour and the learning of new facts and concepts.*

(Peacock, 2006)

You should consider why these two evaluations, which actually both contain evidence which is contradictory, on the one hand give an overall 'little impact', and on the other a 'significant impact' assessment. Key questions you should ask yourself are 'In what terms was the impact measured?' and 'What indicators of impact were considered?'.

The first of these questions is usually contained at the start of any evaluation report, and provides the terms and scope of the evaluation. Without knowing this, the report is actually difficult to understand.

Action Point

Access Alan Peacock's report (available at **www.nationaltrust.org.uk/main/w-schools-guardianships-changing_minds.pdf**), and read the executive summary. Discuss with your HEI tutor the extent to which the findings are presented in terms which are compatible with the stated objectives of the study.

Planning and starting an enquiry
Now that some of the key concepts have been discussed, we can start to look at the steps in planning and undertaking your project. You should spend some time with your coach and HEI tutor discussing your possible focus, and making sure that the enquiry is something you can actually undertake successfully, and that you will have whatever support you need in doing it. As a brief overview, you need to consider the following steps.

Ensure that the project you choose is one you will enjoy
This may seem a rather strange guideline at first, but remember that you will be doing this piece of work for quite some time – possibly a year. Given this, and given that you may have thought of a number of things which might make a good research project, or indeed may have had some suggested to you, it is helpful in deciding, to consider how much you will personally enjoy undertaking it. Choosing something that will have a clear impact on your own professional practice and also on the children you teach can be a deeply rewarding experience, and having the opportunity to actually assess and evidence this impact is a significant developmental opportunity.

Ensure that the project you choose is manageable
This is not as simplistic a statement as you may think. More research projects come to grief because they are too broad in scope, rather than because they are too narrow. When you work at master's level, the depth of your critical engagement with both evidence and theoretical perspectives is a key issue in your reaching the appropriate level of work. As before, discussing this with a coach and tutor, and indeed, your colleagues, will help you establish the possible scope of your enquiry, and identify any area where it might 'overspill',

or where it might take longer than you have actually planned to collate and assess evidence to address your objectives.

Ensure that the project you choose is viable

Conversely, you also need to ensure that whatever project you choose will last long enough and generate enough evidence for your analysis. This is generally not much of a problem in today's educational environment, but still an important consideration for you.

Ensure that you know how to undertake and report research

Your tutor will have experience of supervising many other students who have engaged in enquiries and research into their practice, and the assessment of its impact. It is possible that they will at this stage offer some tutorial and/or workshop support for you and your colleagues. Increasingly, this type of support is also offered through the university virtual learning environment, so that you can access it at a time that suits you and your personal and professional commitments. They will also discuss with you the ethical protocols involved in undertaking your study.

Ensure that you have permission to carry out the project

You should talk to your head teacher about the project you wish to carry out, as it is vital that you have permission, not only to carry out the research, but also to have access to particular sources of evidence. Another key reason why you should negotiate this with your head teacher is that it is often possible that the research you want to carry out may link in with existing school development and improvement plans, and as such, the support of your head teacher and other colleagues will be invaluable. There may also be ethical issues (explored next) within your research which you will need to discuss with the head teacher at the outset.

Ensure that the project you choose adheres to a set of ethical principles

In undertaking practice-based or practitioner research, you will be dealing with some young and vulnerable people. You need to ensure that you do more in terms of exploring ethical considerations than simply anonymising them and the name of your school in your report. Issues of consent are often problematic in such an environment. Chapter 2 discusses in more detail some of the ethical considerations in research and you should reread this before planning your final enquiry.

Assignments

Suggested assignments for phase 3

This last phase requires you to do two 30-credits assignments. The first of these will involve some type of review of cutting-edge practice and/or theory. Some suggested approaches to this assignment are as follows.

- Select an area of your practice that you would like to know more about, and plan and carry out a review of relevant recent literature and research reports. Present this as an annotated bibliography in the style recommended by your HEI.
- Find out what collaborative opportunities are available to you, and plan the way in which you will focus, record and analyse the benefits of your collaborative experience. Collect all the evidence in a portfolio, supported by a critically reflective account of your learning.
- Seek permission to shadow the work of a senior manager, and compile a report of the nature and scope of their work, based on a theoretical understanding of management theory.

The second assignment will involve you undertaking a practice-based enquiry. Some suggested approaches are as follows.

- Having read the report cited earlier of the National Trust Guardianship Scheme evaluation, plan and carry out a formal evaluation of some initiative that you and your colleagues are involved in. Compile a formal report at the end.
- Read some of the chapters from *Teachers Investigate Their Work: An introduction to action research across the professions*, by Altrichter *et al.,* (2008) and plan and carry out an evaluation of your own classroom practice, and subsequent attempt to improve it. Make sure you can support any claims for improvement that you make.
- Undertake a small-scale action research project with some colleagues, and prepare a report of its outcome in a format suitable to present as a professional development session for other teachers. You may support this presentation with annotated video-clips of practice, mini case studies, etc. as you see appropriate.

Summary

At the end of this chapter you should have:
- a systematic understanding of how to access, interpret, use and apply research;
- learned to communicate clearly your conclusions to specialist and non-specialist audiences in your schools and beyond;
- developed ideas for engaging in collaborative learning opportunities in your specialist professional fields and through planning for further professional development;
- learned how to design, carry out and critically analyse a master's-level, practice-based enquiry in your specialist professional field, which explores relationships between theoretical and practical knowledge, and impacts on practice.

Further reading

The Journal of Reflective Practice, published by Taylor and Francis.
Educational Action Research Journal, published by Taylor and Francis.
Green, K. (1999) Defining the field of literature in action research: a personal approach. *Educational Action Research*, 7 (1).

Useful websites

Leading Edge **www.ledge.org.uk**
Purdue Online Writing Lab **http://owl.english.purdue.edu/owl/**
Jack Whitehead's site **www.actionresearch.net/**

End words

When you embarked on your MTL, you were entering into a period of professional development, which hopefully will have illustrated to you the importance of continued learning in your professional practice. Just as your ITT qualification did not complete your education as a teacher, neither does your MTL. One of the aims of phase 3 of the MTL is *providing a basis for the next stage in...professional development*. As such then, while your new master's qualification marks a significant milestone in your professional learning, and is something you can rightly be proud of, you should also be much more proactive in making decisions about your ongoing learning needs.

It is possible that during your studies, you may have uncovered your leadership potential, and wish to further develop this capacity. On the other hand, it may be that you have discovered a flair for supporting your colleagues in their professional development, or a particular strength in subject- or phase-related pedagogy, or in multi-professional work. There are many opportunities available to you to take these interests and emerging expertise further. Of particular interest to many teachers are the opportunities provided by the National College for Leadership of Schools and Children's Services (formerly the National College for School Leadership). Other opportunities can be found through the TDA and DCSF websites, or subject associations. Having completed your MTL, and had significant input into its shaping to suit your own context and circumstances, you are now well equipped to undertake the identification and planning of your own continuing professional development throughout your teaching career.

We wish you every success in your MTL, and future career.

Mary McAteer

Appendix 1 Professional standards mapped for progression by content area

Progression table for Chapter 3

QTS	Core	Post-threshold	Excellent	Advanced skills
			Identified progression ➤	
2. Professional knowledge and understanding				
Q10 Have a knowledge and understanding of a range of teaching, learning and behaviour management strategies and know how to use and adapt them, including how to personalise learning and provide opportunities for all learners to achieve their potential	**C10** Have a good, up-to-date working knowledge and understanding of a range of teaching, learning and behaviour management strategies and know how to use and adapt them, including how to personalise learning to provide opportunities for all learners to achieve their potential	**P2** Have an extensive knowledge and understanding of how to use and adapt a range of teaching, learning and behaviour management strategies, including how to personalise learning to provide opportunities	**E3** Have a critical understanding of the most effective teaching, learning and behaviour management strategies, including how to select and use approaches that personalise learning to provide opportunities for all learners to achieve their potential	
Q11 Know the assessment requirements and arrangements for the subjects/curriculum areas they are trained to teach, including those relating to public examinations and qualifications.	**C11** Know the assessment requirements and arrangements for the subjects/curriculum areas they teach, including those relating to public examinations and qualifications	**P3** Have an extensive knowledge and well-informed understanding of the assessment requirements and arrangements for the subjects/curriculum areas they teach, including those related to public examinations and qualifications **P4** Have up-to-date knowledge and understanding of the different types of qualifications and specifications and their suitability for meeting learners' needs		

Q	C	E
Q12 Know a range of approaches to assessment, including the importance of formative assessment	**C12** Know a range of approaches to assessment, including the importance of formative assessment	
Q13 Know how to use local and national statistical information to evaluate the effectiveness of their teaching, to monitor the progress of those they teach and to raise levels of attainment	**C13** Know how to use local and national statistical information to evaluate the effectiveness of their teaching, to monitor the progress of those they teach and to raise levels of attainment	
	C14 Know how to use reports and other sources of external information related to assessment in order to provide learners with accurate and constructive feedback on their strengths, weaknesses, attainment, progress and areas for development, including action plans for improvement	**E4** Know how to improve the effectiveness of assessment practice in the workplace, including how to analyse statistical information to evaluate the effectiveness of teaching and learning across the school
3. Professional skills		
Q26 (a) Make effective use of a range of assessment, monitoring and recording strategies. (b) Assess the learning needs of those they teach in order to set challenging learning objectives	**C31** Make effective use of an appropriate range of observation, assessment, monitoring and recording strategies as a basis for setting challenging learning objectives and monitoring learners' progress and levels of attainment	**E10** Demonstrate excellent ability to assess and evaluate
Q27 Provide learners, colleagues, parents and carers with timely, accurate and constructive feedback on learners' attainment, progress and areas for development	**C32** Provide learners, colleagues, parents and carers with timely, accurate and constructive feedback on learners' attainment, progress and areas for development	**E11** Have an excellent ability to provide learners, colleagues, parents and carers with timely, accurate and constructive feedback on learners' attainment, progress and areas for development that promotes pupil progress
Q28 Support and guide learners to reflect on their learning, identify the progress they have made and identify their emerging learning needs	**C33** Support and guide learners so that they can reflect on their learning, identify the progress they have made, set positive targets for improvement and become successful independent learners	
	C34 Use assessment as part of their teaching to diagnose learners' needs, set realistic and challenging targets for improvement and plan future teaching	

Progression table for Chapter 4

QTS	Core	Post-threshold	Excellent	Advanced skills
		Identified progression →		
Q3 (a) Be aware of the professional duties of teachers and the statutory framework within which they work (b) Be aware of the policies and practices of the workplace and share in collective responsibility for their implementation		**C3** Maintain an up-to-date knowledge and understanding of the professional duties of teachers and the statutory framework within which they work, and contribute to the development, implementation and evaluation of the policies and practice of their workplace, including those designed to promote equality of opportunity		
			P1 Contribute significantly, where appropriate, to implementing workplace policies and practice and to promoting collective responsibility for their implementation	
			E1 Be willing to take a leading role in developing workplace policies and practice and in promoting collective responsibility for their implementation	**A1** Be willing to take on a strategic leadership role in developing workplace policies and practice and in promoting collective responsibility for their implementation in their own and other workplaces

2. Professional knowledge and understanding

Q	C	P	E
Q14 Have a secure knowledge and understanding of their subjects/curriculum areas and related pedagogy to enable them to teach effectively across the age and ability range for which they are trained	**C15** Have a secure knowledge and understanding of their subjects/curriculum areas and related pedagogy including: the contribution that their subjects/curriculum areas can make to cross-curricular learning; and recent relevant developments	**P5** Have a more developed knowledge and understanding of their subjects/curriculum areas and related pedagogy including how learning progresses within them	**E5** Have an extensive and deep knowledge and understanding of their subjects/curriculum areas and related pedagogy gained for example through involvement in wider professional networks associated with their subjects/curriculum areas
Q14 Have a secure knowledge and understanding of their subjects/curriculum areas and related pedagogy to enable them to teach effectively across the age and ability range for which they are trained	**C16** Know and understand the relevant statutory and non-statutory curricula and frameworks, including those provided through the National Strategies, for their subjects/curriculum areas and other relevant initiatives across the age and ability range they teach		
Q15 Know and understand the relevant statutory and non-statutory curricula and frameworks, including those provided through the National Strategies, for their subjects/curriculum areas, and other relevant initiatives applicable to the age and ability range for which they are trained	**C17** Know how to use skills in literacy, numeracy and ICT to support their teaching and wider professional activities		

3. Professional skills

Q	C	E
Q23 Design opportunities for learners to develop their literacy, numeracy and ICT skills	Design opportunities for learners to develop their literacy, numeracy	**C27** Design opportunities for learners to develop their literacy, numeracy, ICT and thinking and learning skills appropriate within their phase and context

Progression table for Chapter 5

QTS	Core	Post-threshold	Excellent	Advanced skills
			Identified progression →	
1. Professional attributes				
Q1 Have high expectations of children and young people including a commitment to ensuring that they can achieve their full educational potential and to establishing fair, respectful, trusting, supportive and constructive relationships with them	**C1** Have high expectations of children and young people including a commitment to ensuring that they can achieve their full educational potential and to establishing fair, respectful, trusting, supportive and constructive relationships with them			
Q2 Demonstrate the positive values, attitudes and behaviour they expect from children and young people	**C2** Hold positive values and attitudes and adopt high standards of behaviour in their professional role			
Q4 Communicate effectively with children, young people, colleagues, parents and carers	**C4** (a) Communicate effectively with children, young people and colleagues (b) Communicate effectively with parents and carers, conveying timely and relevant information about attainment, objectives, progress and well-being (c) Recognise that communication is a two-way process and encourage parents and carers to participate in discussions about the progress, development and well-being of children and young people			
Q5 Recognise and respect the contribution that colleagues, parents and carers can make to the development and well-being of children and young people, and to raising their levels of attainment	**C5** Recognise and respect the contributions that colleagues, parents and carers can make to the development and well-being of children and young people, and to raising their levels of attainment			
Q7 (a) Reflect on and improve their practice, and take responsibility for identifying and meeting their developing professional needs	**C7** Evaluate their performance and be committed to improving their practice through appropriate professional development			

2. Professional knowledge and understanding

Q10 Have a knowledge and understanding of a range of teaching, learning and behaviour management strategies and know how to use and adapt them, including how to personalise learning and provide opportunities for all learners to achieve their potential	C10 Have a good, up-to-date working knowledge and understanding of a range of teaching, learning and behaviour management strategies and know how to use and adapt them, including how to personalise learning to provide opportunities for all learners to achieve their potential	
	P2 Have an extensive knowledge and understanding of how to use and adapt a range of teaching, learning and behaviour management strategies, including how to personalise learning to provide opportunities for all learners to achieve their potential	
		E3 Have a critical understanding of the most effective teaching, learning and behaviour management strategies, including how to select and use approaches that personalise learning to provide opportunities for all learners to achieve their potential
Q18 Understand how children and young people develop and that the progress and well-being of learners are affected by a range of developmental, social, religious, ethnic, cultural and linguistic influences	C18 Understand how children and young people develop and how the progress, rate of development and well-being of learners are affected by a range of developmental, social, religious, ethnic, cultural and linguistic influences	
Q19 Know how to make effective personalised provision for those they teach, including those for whom English is an additional language or who have special educational needs or disabilities, and how to take practical account of diversity and promote equality and inclusion in their teaching	C19 Know how to make effective personalised provision for those they teach, including those for whom English is an additional language or who have special educational needs or disabilities, and how to take practical account of diversity and promote equality and inclusion in their teaching	
		E6 Have an extensive knowledge on matters concerning equality, inclusion and diversity in teaching
Q21 (b) Know how to identify and support children and young people whose progress, development or well-being is affected by changes or difficulties in their personal circumstances, and when to refer them to colleagues for specialist support	C24 Know how to identify potential child abuse or neglect and follow safeguarding procedures	
	C25 Know how to identify and support children and young people whose progress, development or well-being is affected by changes or difficulties in their personal circumstances, and when to refer them to colleagues for specialist support	
	P6 Have sufficient depth of knowledge and experience to be able to give advice on the development and well-being of children and young people	

3. Professional skills

Q31 Establish a clear framework for classroom discipline to manage learners' behaviour constructively and promote their self-control and independence	C38 (a) Manage learners' behaviour constructively by establishing and maintaining a clear and positive framework for discipline, in line with the school's behaviour policy (b) Use a range of behaviour management techniques and strategies, adapting them as necessary to promote the self-control and independence of learners C39 Promote learners' self-control, independence and co-operation through developing their social, emotional and behavioural skills	

Progression table for Chapter 6

QTS	Core	Post-threshold	Excellent	Advanced skills
			Identified progression →	
1. Professional attributes				
Q5 Recognise and respect the contribution that colleagues, parents and carers can make to the development and well-being of children and young people and to raising their levels of attainment	C5 Recognise and respect the contributions that colleagues, parents and carers can make to the development and well-being of children and young people, and to raising their levels of attainment			
Q6 Have a commitment to collaboration and co-operative working	C6 Have a commitment to collaboration and co-operative working where appropriate			
				E1 Be willing to take a leading role in developing workplace policies and practice and in promoting collective responsibility for their implementation
2. Professional knowledge and understanding				
Q20 Know and understand the roles of colleagues with specific responsibilities, including those with responsibility for learners with special educational needs and disabilities and other individual learning needs	C20 Understand the roles of colleagues such as those having specific responsibilities for learners with special educational needs, disabilities and other individual learning needs, and the contributions they can make to the learning, development and well-being of children and young people			
	C21 Know when to draw on the expertise of colleagues, such as those with responsibility for the safeguarding of children and young people and special educational needs and disabilities, and to refer to sources of information, advice and support from external agencies			
Q21 (a) Be aware of the current legal requirements, national policies and guidance on the safeguarding and promotion of the well-being of children and young people	C22 Know the current legal requirements, national policies and guidance on the safeguarding and promotion of the well-being of children and young people			
	C23 Know the local arrangements concerning the safeguarding of children and young people			
	C24 Know how to identify potential child abuse or neglect and follow safeguarding procedures			
	C25 Know how to identify and support children and young people whose progress, development or well-being is affected by changes or difficulties in their personal circumstances, and when to refer them to colleagues for specialist support			
				E7 (a) Take a lead in planning collaboratively with colleagues in order to promote effective practice

3. Professional skills

Q	C	P	E	A
Q30 Establish a purposeful and safe learning environment conducive to learning and identify opportunities for learners to learn in out-of-school contexts	**C37** (a) Establish a purposeful and safe learning environment which complies with current legal requirements, national policies and guidance on the safeguarding and well being of children and young people so that learners feel secure and sufficiently confident to make an active contribution to learning and to the school (b) Make use of the local arrangements concerning the safeguarding of children and young people (c) Identify and use opportunities to personalise and extend learning through out-of-school contexts where possible making links between in-school learning and learning in out-of-school contexts			
Q32 Work as a team member and identify opportunities for working with colleagues, sharing the development of effective practice with them	**C40** Work as a team member and identify opportunities for working with colleagues, managing their work where appropriate and sharing the development of effective practice with them	**P9** Promote collaboration and work effectively as a team member	**E13** Work closely with leadership teams, taking a leading role in developing, implementing and evaluating policies and practice that contribute to school improvement	**A2** Be part of or work closely with leadership teams, taking a leadership role in developing, implementing and evaluating policies and practice in their own and other workplaces that contribute to school improvement
Q33 Ensure that colleagues working with them are appropriately involved in supporting learning and understand the roles they are expected to fulfil	**C41** Ensure that colleagues working with them are appropriately involved in supporting learning and understand the roles they are expected to fulfil	**P10** Contribute to the professional development of colleagues through coaching and mentoring, demonstrating effective practice, and providing advice and feedback	**E14** Contribute to the professional development of colleagues using a broad range of techniques and skills appropriate to their needs so that they demonstrate enhanced and effective practice **E15** Make well-founded appraisals of situations upon which they are asked to advise, applying high-level skills in classroom observation to evaluate and advise colleagues on their work and devising and implementing effective strategies to meet the learning needs of children and young people leading to improvements in pupil outcomes	**A3** Possess the analytical, interpersonal and organisational skills necessary to work effectively with staff and leadership teams beyond their own school

Progression table for Chapter 7

Identified progression → (toward Advanced skills)

QTS	Core	Post-threshold	Excellent	Advanced skills
Professional attributes				
Q7 (a) Reflect on and improve their practice, and take responsibility for identifying and meeting their developing professional needs (b) Identify priorities for their early professional development		C7 Evaluate their performance and be committed to improving their practice through appropriate professional development		
Q8 Have a creative and constructively critical approach towards innovation, being prepared to adapt their practice where benefits and improvements are identified		C8 Have a creative and constructively critical approach towards innovation; being prepared to adapt their practice where benefits and improvements are identified	E2 Research and evaluate innovative curricular practices and draw on research outcomes and other sources of external evidence to inform their own practice and that of colleagues	
Q9 Act upon advice and feedback and be open to coaching and mentoring		C9 Act upon advice and feedback and be open to coaching and mentoring		
Professional skills				
Q29 Evaluate the impact of their teaching on the progress of all learners, and modify their planning and classroom practice where necessary		C35 Review the effectiveness of their teaching and its impact on learners' progress, attainment and well-being, refining their approaches where necessary		
Q32 Work as a team member and identify opportunities for working with colleagues, sharing the development of effective practice with them		C40 Work as a team member and identify opportunities for working with colleagues, managing their work where appropriate and sharing the development of effective practice with them		

Appendix 2 QAA guide to master's-level qualifications

Master's level
Much of the study undertaken at master's-level will have been at, or informed by, the forefront of an academic or professional discipline. Students will have shown originality in the application of knowledge, and they will understand how the boundaries of knowledge are advanced through research. They will be able to deal with complex issues both systematically and creatively, and they will show originality in tackling and solving problems.

They will have the qualities needed for employment in circumstances requiring sound judgement, personal responsibility and initiative, in complex and unpredictable professional environments.

Master's degrees are awarded after completion of taught courses, programmes of research, or a mixture of both. Longer, research-based programmes often lead to the degree of MPhil. Most master's courses last at least one year (if taken full-time), and are taken by persons with honours degrees (or equivalent achievement). Some master's degrees in science and engineering are awarded after extended undergraduate programmes that last, typically, a year longer than honours degree programmes. Also at this level are advanced short courses, often forming parts of continuing professional development programmes, leading to postgraduate certificates and postgraduate diplomas.

Descriptor for a qualification at master's (M) level: master's degree
Master's degrees are awarded to students who have demonstrated:
1. a systematic understanding of knowledge, and a critical awareness of current problems and/or new insights, much of which is at, or informed by, the forefront of their academic discipline, field of study, or area of professional practice;
2. a comprehensive understanding of techniques applicable to their own research or advanced scholarship;
3. originality in the application of knowledge, together with a practical understanding of how established techniques of research and enquiry are used to create and interpret knowledge in the discipline;
4. conceptual understanding that enables the student:
   - to evaluate critically current research and advanced scholarship in the discipline; and
   - to evaluate methodologies and develop critiques of them and, where appropriate, to propose new hypotheses.

Typically, holders of the qualification will be able to:
a. deal with complex issues both systematically and creatively, make sound judgements in the absence of complete data, and communicate their conclusions clearly to specialist and non-specialist audiences;
b. demonstrate self-direction and originality in tackling and solving problems, and act autonomously in planning and implementing tasks at a professional or equivalent level;

c. continue to advance their knowledge and understanding, and to develop new skills to a high level;

and will have:

d. the qualities and transferable skills necessary for employment requiring:

the exercise of initiative and personal responsibility;

decision-making in complex and unpredictable situations; and

the independent learning ability required for continuing professional development.

References

Allen, J. (2008) *Rethinking Inclusive Education: The philosophers of difference in practice.* Dordrecht: Springer.

Altrichter, A., Feldman, A., Posch, P. and Somekh, B. (2008) *Teachers Investigate Their Work: A an introduction to action research across the professions.* Abingdon: Routledge.

Andrews, R. (2003) *What Counts as Evidence in Education?* Available at **www.ttrb.ac.uk/ attachments/38ba1867-f5d9-4c5f-943c-3218a7399724.pdf**

Anning, A., Cottrell, D., Frost, N., Green, J. and Robinson, M. (2006) *Developing Multiprofessional Teamwork for Integrated Children's Services.* Maidenhead: Open University Press/McGraw-Hill.

Assessment Reform Group (1999) *Assessment for Learning: Beyond the Black Box.* Cambridge: University of Cambridge School of Education.

Bassey, M. (1999) *Case Study Research in Educational Settings.* Buckingham: Open University Press.

BERA (2004) *Revised Ethical Guidelines for Educational Research.* Nottingham: BERA.

Black, P., Harrison, C., Lee, C., Marshall, B. and Wiliam, D. (2003) *Assessment for Learning: Putting it into practice.* Maidenhead: Open University Press/McGraw-Hill.

Blandford, S. (2006) *Middle Leadership in Schools.* Harlow: Pearson Education.

Booth, T. and Ainscow, M., (2002) *Index for Inclusion: Developing learning and participation in schools.* Bristol: CSIE.

Brennan, W.K. (1982) *Special Education in Mainstream Schools: The Search for Quality.* Stratford Upon Avon: National Council for Special Education.

Brookfield, S. (1995) *Becoming A Critically Reflective Teacher.* San Francisco, CA: Jossey-Bass.

Burton, D. and Bartlett, S. (2009) *Key Issues for Education Researchers* London: Sage.

Bush, T. (2008) *Leadership and Management Development in Education.* London: Sage.

Bush, T. and Glover, D. (2003) *School Leadership: Concepts and Evidence.* Nottingham: NCSL.

Bush, T. and Middlewood, D. (2005) *Leading and Managing People in Education.* London: Sage.

Castle, K. (2009) *Study Skills for your Master's in Teaching and Learning.* Exeter: Learning Matters.

Children Act (2004) London: HMSO.

Christensen, P. and James, A. (2000) *Research with Children: Perspectives and practice.* Abingdon: Falmer Press.

Clarke, S. (1998) *Targeting Assessment in the Primary Classroom,* London: Hodder & Stoughton.

Clarke, S. (2001) *Unlocking Formative Assessment – Practical strategies for enhancing pupils' learning in the primary classroom.* London: Hodder & Stoughton.

Clarke, S. (2003) *Enriching Feedback in the Primary Classroom.* London: Hodder & Stoughton.

Coe, R., Fitz-Gibbon, C. and Tymms, P. (2002) *Promoting Evidence-Based Education: The role of practitioners,* Round table discussion, BERA 2002.

Cole, T. (2005) Policies for positive behaviour management, in K. Topping and S. Maloney (eds) *The RoutledgeFalmer Reader in Inclusive Education.* Abingdon: RoutledgeFalmer.

Cooper, P. (1994) *Emotional and Behavioural Difficulties: Theory to practice.* Abingdon: Routledge-Falmer.

Cuban, L. (1988) *The Managerial Imperative and the Practice of Leadership in School.* Albany, New York: State University of New York Press.

Davies, B. (2009) *The Essentials of School Leadership.* London: Sage.

DCSF (2007a) *The Children's Plan: Building Brighter Futures.* Norwich: The Stationery Office.

DCSF (2007b) *The Primary Framework.* London: DCSF.

DCSF (2008) *Being the Best for Our Children: Releasing talent for teaching and learning*. Available at **http://publiations.gov.uk**

DCSF (2008a) *Revised Guidance on the Education of Children and Young People with Behavioural, Emotional and Social Difficulties*. (BESD) London: DCSF.

DCSF (2008b) *Statutory Guidance on Induction for Newly Qualified Teachers in England*. London: DCSF.

DCSF (2008c) *21st Century Schools: A world class education for every child*. Nottingham: DCSF.

DCSF (2008d) *The Impact of Parental Involvement on Children's Education*. Nottingham: DCSF.

DCSF (2009) *Your Child, Your Schools, Our Future: Building a 21st Century Schools System*. Norwich: The Stationery Office.

Demos (2008) *About Learning*. London: Demos.

DES (1989) *Discipline in Schools: Report of the Committee of Enquiry* (The Elton Report). London: HMSO.

DfEE (1997) *Excellence for All Children: Meeting special educational needs*. London: DfEE.

DfES (2001) *Inclusive Schooling*. London: DfES.

DfES (2003) *Every Child Matters*. Norwich: HMSO.

DfES (2004a) *Removing Barriers to Achievement: The Government Strategy*. London: DfES.

DfES (2004b) *Every Child Matters: Change for Children in Schools*. London: DfES.

DfES (2005a) *Common Core of Skills and Knowledge for the Children's Workforce*. Nottingham: DfES.

DfES (2005b) *Harnessing Technology: Transforming learning and children's services*. London: DfES.

DfES (2005c) *Learning Behaviour: The Report of the Practitioners Group on School Behaviour and Discipline* (The Steer Report). London: DfES.

DfES (2006a) *Independent Review of the Teaching of Early Reading*. London: DfES.

DfES (2006b) *Select Committee Report on Special Educational Needs*. London: DfES.

Disability Discrimination Act (DDA) (1995) London: HMSO.

Dunn, R. and Dunn, K. (1978) *Teaching Students Through Their Individual Learning Styles: A practical approach*. Virginia: Reston Publishing.

Education Act (1996) London: HMSO.

Education and Inspection Act (2006) London: HMSO.

Elliott, J. (1991) *Action Research for Educational Change*. Buckingham: Open University Press.

Endacott, R., Gray, M., Jasper, M., McMullan, M., Miller, C., Scholes, J. and Webb, C. (2004) Using portfolios in the assessment of learning and competence: the impact of four models. *Nurse Education in Practice*, 4: 250–7.

Everard, K.B., Morris, G. and Wilson, I. (2004) *Effective School Management*. London: Sage.

French, J. and Raven, B. (1959) Bases of social power, in Cartwright, D. (ed.) *Studies in Social Power*. Ann Arbor, MI: University of Michigan.

GTC (2007) *Making CPD better*, available at **www.gtce.org.uk/documents/publicationpdfs/ tplf_better_tp070107.pdf**

Gipps, C. (1994) *Beyond Testing: Towards a theory of educational assessment*. Abingdon: Falmer Press.

Harlen, W. (1994) *Enhancing Quality in Assessment*. London: Paul Chapman Publishing.

Harlen, W. and Schlapp, U. (1998) *Literature Reviews*. Available at **http://www.scre.ac.uk/spotlight/ spotlight71.html**

Harris, D. and Bell, C. (1994) *Evaluating and Assessing for Learning* (revised edition). London: Kogan Page.

Hopkins, D., Higham, R. and Ahtaridou, E. (2009) *School Leadership in England: Contemporary challenges, innovative responses and future trends*. Nottingham: NCSL.

Howes, C. and Ritchie, S. (2002) *A Matter of Trust: Connecting teachers and learners in the early childhood classroom*. New York: New York Teachers College Press.

Hughes, P. (2005) Learning mentors in primary classrooms and schools, in Campbell, A. and

Fairbairn, G. (eds) *Working with Support in the Classroom*. London: Paul Chapman Publishing.

Hughes, W. (2000) *Critical Thinking: An introduction to the basic skills*. Peterborough, Ont.: Broadview Press.

Kemmis, S. and McTaggart, R. (1981) *The Action Research Planner*. Victoria: Deakin University Press.

Leithwood, K., Day, C., Sammons, P., Harris, A. and Hopkins, D. (2006) *Seven Strong Claims about Successful School Leadership*. London: Department for Education and Skills.

MacBeath, J. (ed.) (1998) *Effective School Leadership*. London: Paul Chapman Publishing/Sage.

McCreery, E., Palmer, S. and Voiels, V. (2008) *Teaching Religious Education: Primary and early years*. Exeter: Learning Matters.

Mason, J. (2002) *Researching Your Own Practice: The discipline of noticing*. Abingdon: RoutledgeFalmer.

Moon, J. (2006) *Learning Journals: A handbook for reflective practice and professional development*. Abingdon: RoutledgeFalmer.

Moon, J. (2008) *Critical Thinking: An exploration of theory and practice*. Abingdon: Routledge.

Northouse, P. (2009) *Introduction to Leadership Concepts and Practice*. London: Sage.

Ofsted (Office for Standards in Education) (2005) *Managing Challenging Behaviour*. HMI 2363. London: Ofsted.

Ofsted (Office for Standards in Education) (2005) *Improving Behaviour*. London: Ofsted.

Open University: *Skills for OU Study*. **www.open.ac.uk/skillsforstudy/critical-thinking.php**

Osterman, K. and Kottkamp, R. (2004) *Reflective Practice for Educators: Professional development to improve student learning*. London: Sage.

Papatheodorou, T. (2005) *Behaviour Problems in the Early Years: A guide for understanding and support*. Abingdon: Routledge Falmer.

Paris, S. and Winograd, P. (1990) How metacognition can promote academic learning and instruction, in B. Jones and L. Idol (eds) *Dimensions of Thinking and Cognitive Instruction*. Hillsdale, NJ: Lawrence Erlbaum Associates.

Parton, N. (2006) *Safeguarding Childhood: Early intervention and surveillance in a late modern society*. Basingstoke: Palgrave Macmillan.

Peacock, A. (2006) Changing Minds: The lasting impact of school trips. University of Exeter, The Innovation Centre, available at **www.nationaltrust.org.uk/main/w-schools-guardianships-changing_minds.pdf**

Pollard, A. (1997) *Reflective Teaching in the Primary School* (3rd edn). London: Cassell.

Poulson L. and Wallace M. (2004) *Learning to Read Critically in Teaching and Learning*. London: Sage.

Pring, R. (2000) *Philosophy of Educational Research*. London: Continuum.

Reis, R. M. (2009) *What Makes a Good Teacher*, available at **www.mnsu.edu/cetl/teaching resources/articles/goodteacher.html** (accessed 1 June 2009).

Richert, A. (1991) Case methods and teacher education: Using cases to develop teach teacher reflection, in B. Tabachnick and K. Zeichner (eds) *Issues and Practices in Inquiry-orientated Teacher Education* (130–50). New York: RoutledgeFalmer.

Ridley, D. (2008) *The Literature Review: A step-by-step guide for students*, London: Sage.

Riel, M. (2007) *Understanding Action Research*. Center For Collaborative Action Research. Available at **http://cadres.pepperdine.edu/ccar/define.html**

Rogers, C.R. (1947) Some Observations on the Organization of Personality. *American Psychologist*, 2: 358–68.

Rogers, C.R. (1951) *Client-centered Therapy: Its current practice, implications and theory*. London: Constable.

Rogers, C.R. (1959) A theory of therapy, personality and interpersonal relationships as developed in the client-centered framework, in S. Koch (ed.) *Psychology: A Study of a Science. Vol. 3: Formulations of the Person and the Social Context*. New York: McGraw-Hill.

Russell, T. (2002) Can self-study improve teacher education?, in Loughran, J. and Russell, T. (eds)

Improving Teacher Education Practices Through Self-study. Abingdon: RoutledgeFalmer.

Rustemeir, S. (2002) *The Inclusion Charter*. Bristol: Centre for Studies on Inclusive Education.

Rycroft-Malone J., Seers K., Titchen, A., Harvey, G., Kitson, A. and McCormack, B. (2004) What counts as evidence in evidence-based practice. *Journal of Advanced Nursing*, 47: 81–90.

Special Educational Needs and Disability Act (SENDA) (2001) London: HMSO.

Sadler, R. (1989) Formative assessment and the design of instructional systems. *Instructional Science*, 18: 119–44.

Schön, D. (1983) *The Reflective Practitioner*. London: Temple Smith.

Senge, P., Scharmer, C.O., Jaworski, J. and Flowers, B.S. (2004) *Presence*. Cambridge, MA: Society of Organizational Learning.

Sergiovanni, T.J. (1984) Leadership and excellence in schooling. *Educational Leadership*, 41(5): 4–13.

Smith, M.K. (2001) Donald Schön: learning, reflection and change, in *The Encyclopedia of Informal Education*. Available at **www.infed.org/thinkers/et-schon.htm**

Somekh, B. (2007) *Pedagogy and Learning with ICT*. Abingdon: Routledge.

Stake, R.E. (1995) *The Art of Case Study Research*. London: Sage.

Stark, R. (1998) *Practitioner Research: The purposes of reviewing the literature within an enquiry*. Available: **http://www.scre.ac.uk/spotlight/spotlight67.html**.

Stiggins, R.J. (2002) Assessment crisis: The absence of assessment for learning. *Phi Delta Kappan*, June, 758–765.

TDA (2009) *The National Framework for Masters in Teaching and Learning*. London: TDA.

Thomas, G. and Loxley, A. (2001) *Deconstructing Special Education and Constructing Inclusion*. Buckingham: Open University Press.

Todd, L. (2007) *Partnerships for Inclusive Education: A critical approach to collaborative working*. Abingdon.: Routledge.

UNESCO (1960) Convention Against Discrimination in Education (1960). Paris: UNESCO.

UNESCO (1994) The Salamanca Statement and Framework on Special Needs Education. Paris: UNESCO

United Nations (1989) Convention on the Rights of the Child. New York: UN.

United Nations (2007) Convention on the Rights of Persons with Disabilities. New York: UN.

University of Winsconsin Writing Center **http://writing.wisc.edu/Handbook/Annotated Bibliography.html**

Usher, R.S. and Bryant, I. (1989) *Adult Education as Theory, Practice and Research: The captive triangle*. New York: Routledge.

Vincett, K., Cremin, H. and Thomas, G. (2005) *Teachers and Assistants Working Together*. Maidenhead: Open University Press/McGraw-Hill.

Violent Crime Reduction Act (2006) London: HMSO.

Walker, S. and Thurston, C. (2006) *Safeguarding Children and Young People: A guide to integrated practice*. Lyme Regis: Russell House.

Weeden, P., Winter, J. and Broadfoot, P. (2002) *Assessment. What's in it for schools?* Abingdon: RoutledgeFalmer.

West-Burnham, J. (1977) *Managing Quality in Schools*. Abingdon: Falmer Press.

Whitehead, J. (2003) *What Counts as Evidence in Self-Studies of Teacher Education Practices?* Available at **http://www.actionresearch.net/writings/evid.htm**

Winter, R. (1987) *Action Research and the Nature of Social Inquiry: Professional innovation and educational work*. Aldershot: Avebury.

Index

Added to a page number 'f' denotes a figure and 't' denotes a table.